CHIPS, VIDEOS AND ALCOHOL

CHIPS, VIDEOS AND ALCOHOL

A Father's Guide to Survival

ALAN CHARLTON

NEW HOLLAND

First published in 2005 by New Holland Publishers (UK) Ltd
London • Cape Town • Sydney • Auckland

10 9 8 7 6 5 4 3 2 1

www.newhollandpublishers.com

Garfield House, 86–88 Edgware Road, London W2 2EA, UK

80 McKenzie Street, Cape Town 8001, South Africa

14 Aquatic Drive, Frenchs Forest, NSW 2086, Australia

218 Lake Road, Northcote, Auckland, New Zealand

ISBN 1 84537 117 8

Publishing Manager: Jo Hemmings
Senior Editor: Kate Michell
Assistant Editor: Kate Parker
Design: Gülen Shevki-Taylor
Cover design: Ian Hughes, Mousemat Design Ltd.
Production: Joan Woodroffe

Reproduction by Modern Age Repro House, Hong Kong
Printed and bound by Replika Press PVT Ltd, India

Acknowledgements

'THANKS GLENN'
Karen, many thanks for all your help; your whisky is in the post.
A big thank you to Lorraine for the read through and for being
the only person I've met who knows someone who can eat
pickled eggs. Thanks to Joan Deitch, Helen Simpson, Jamie
O'Keefe and John Helliwell for all their help and support.
To my wonderful Mum and Dad, I understand so much more.

contents

Foreword

Living on a diet of chips, videos and alcohol? Welcome to the life of the househusband. I would like to welcome you, the new father, to the first day of the rest of your life. If you are thinking about taking over the role traditionally given to the mother of staying at home and caring for your children, then get ready for the ride of your life. It's bigger, faster, more infuriating, terrifying and enjoyable than anything you can imagine or dream of. (Well almost! If your daydream is a sun-washed beach full of naked women who lust after your body, and so much money in the bank that they give you a private parking space at the bank's head office, we could have a problem.)

However, this book should help you deal with some of the problems the baby rollercoaster ride can bring you. Its author has been round the whole ride, twice. As with any rollercoaster, you need to strap yourself in for safety and, just like any ride at the theme park, if you don't strap yourself in, it can kill you.

So, read on and see what could be in store for you. Because, with the birth of your baby, you have just made it to the top of the ride – you are going to be heading down fast, with no brakes, and it's going to be a long time before you can get off.

Are you ready to pay the ticket price and get on?

Alan Charlton

Introduction

☎ The Birth of a Book

One thing about telephoning someone with a baby – they might be in the middle of doing something, but you can be sure of one thing: they are always up.

Ring, ring. 'Hi Glenn mate, I thought I would just give you a quick call to see how it's all going. I've just got the screaming little love bundle off to sleep and with his sleeping pattern that gives me about ten minutes' peace to have a coffee and ring you.'

'Well Alan, I don't know… sometimes I just don't get it. He's been a real pain – the little sod won't even stop screaming to give me time to take a piss.'

'I'll tell you what Glenn: we have become sad, miserable gits. We have more chance of winning the lottery than ever understanding what we have to do to make sense of this job. I mean, you get DIY books on painting, plumbing, cooking, fishing and how to give a woman an orgasm, but try and find a book about men, babies and the facts.'

'Well, if there aren't any books, why don't you write one? You can put me down for a copy.'

'Yeah, sure.'

'No, I mean it. I'm sure there are lots of others like us out there. Oh crap! [Sounds of things breaking in the background.] The little monster just pulled over the milk in the fridge. I'll speak to you soon, and in the meantime, think about the book idea – or else we could rob a bank and bugger off somewhere with the money. Oh no! The mess is all over the place. Sorry, mate, got to go. Bye.'

Before the phone went dead, I could feel Glenn's stress building at the other end of the line.

With my coffee still warm, I knew I would not have time to finish it, because I could hear my own little monster waking up in the next room. Yes, another frantic phonecall about the path that we have both taken in our lives. We were faced with seemingly never-ending problems and with how, as men, our women wrapped us round their fingers. Thank God for the calming support of a fellow househusband who understands when you say, 'I'd rather have a filling done by a blind, psychopathic dentist than try to figure out what this screaming bundle of joy wants.'

So it was my good friend and fellow househusband Glenn who first planted the seeds for my writing this book. I hope you enjoy reading as I outline some of the main points about your role as a parent, mother or househusband. As a man writing about looking after a baby, it was a great joy to find that women have the same problems. If you are a man and not the one at home looking after the baby, it will make you appreciate the work your partner puts into looking after the home and the children.

Most of us come from a normal working background: get up, go to work, clock in, have lunch, clock off, go home, bath, shave, meet up with friends, drinks, film, curry: BLISS. Add children to your life and your past becomes a distant memory, which you come to feel must have been from a previous incarnation. When you enter the househusband twilight zone, time takes on a whole new meaning. Albert Einstein had some great ideas on time, but he didn't explain the way children can make a twenty-four-hour day pass in a flash or a single second feel like a week. Before I had children, I had time; finding and handling this precious commodity is the quest only children can send you on. At birth, they may only be seven pounds and fit in one of your hands, but the time warp has begun. This cute little bundle is a time-eating monster and bigger than any time-warp field that Scotty had to deal with on the *Starship Enterprise* or that Albert could ever have imagined.

Rose-tinted specs or elephant bollocks?

So you want to become a househusband?

Do you feel like you want to put the record straight, that men can look after children just as easily as you think women can? What's the big deal? Feed the baby, bit of cleaning, put your feet up, open a beer and watch TV in the afternoon as the baby sleeps off his midday feed. Easy. At the time of writing, my children are seven and eleven. I've been doing the job of househusband since the first one came home from the hospital. 'Easy' is definitely not a word I'd use. Like most people, I had more idea of how to perform a brain operation than I did about looking after a baby, but no-one at the hospital asked for my qualifications when my children were born.

I feel I'm qualified to talk about my experiences of what the job of a full-time father entails because I've been one for so long. Not part-time, not just at weekends. Twenty-four hours a day, seven days a week, 365 days a year, for over eleven years. Or, if you like, 4,015 days, which is 96,360 hours, over five million minutes, or 346 million seconds. If you add the child–time distortion, that makes me 472 years old and I've died at least six times.

In no way is this a 'How-to' book. We are not making a bookcase or doing DIY plumbing; babies are a bigger problem, and we all handle the problems of bringing up children differently. Nor is it a medical textbook. It's just a look at some of the bad, good, bad, happy, sad, bad and fun times of being a househusband. (Yes, I know I said 'bad' more than once, but as you've just started reading I don't want to put you off by using the more colourful words parents sometimes use.)

Let's get one of my biggest headaches about being a parent out in the open, and one you'll have to come to terms with very quickly if you take on the role of househusband. It's the whitewash that begins at the moment of conception or, to put it another way, the rose-tinted specs through which family, friends, films, magazines, books and daytime TV chat shows see 'the wonder of children'. If you are pulling your hair out trying to look after a baby's needs, it's no help other people telling you what a wonderful time you're having. I'll tell you this now: some of the crap that people come out with – about the joy that is now filling their life, for instance – is about as reassuring as signing a contract with a double-glazing salesman. I'm convinced many people go blind about the facts when they look back at bringing up their children; they cannot be honest with themselves and tell the truth. They wouldn't even see how large an elephant's bollocks were if they happened to be walking behind one in the street.

Despite the wonder of a new life in your family, *your* biggest wonder is how to get out of this mess you now find yourself in. Most of the time it feels like a bad dream with only a few seconds of relief when you first wake up in the morning. But soon after comes the realisation that the bad dream is repeating itself. Unlike a bad day at work, you can't walk away for a lunch break or go home sick: you are stuck with it. And it's only 10am.

Watch your parents' faces when you tell them the news about their first grandchild: big smiles all round. But look closely. Is it joy at a new life that is making them smile? Or are they smiling to hold back thunderous laughter, which, if unleashed, would rupture their pancreases and collapse their lungs? Is your father thinking, 'At last, my boy is going to understand?'

Then, filled with the excitement of the moment, you

announce that you're going to stay at home and look after the baby. This is just too much. Your father makes an excuse of having to use the bathroom, feeling his pancreas is about to explode. Your mother, with the protective care of a lioness, hugs her baby boy, maybe hoping to protect you from the unseen dangers of your decision.

Get the idea? This is a no-holds-barred look at what's in store. You may be reading up on the subject at the moment, trying to find out how to look after a baby, trying to find out what to do and how to do it. I feel sure that in time and with hindsight, when you've been a father for a few years, you'd gladly tell the authors of the 'How-to' baby books to go forth and multiply with themselves. Because by then, having done the job, no way are your specs rose-tinted. Your eyes have been opened, you can see the elephant in front of you, and you realise that there is a large pair of bollocks dangling before your eyes.

What the books don't tell you

In all the years I've been doing the job, the hardest part has been akin to the feeling of climbing a mountain in lead boots and reaching the top – only to find it isn't the top. It is a hard, frustrating job, and many of the good times are recognisable as being good only in retrospect.

I've read books and articles about how to control babies' sleeping, what to do about feeding and how to potty train. The only thing wrong with this information was that my children weren't like the ones in the books. And no-one tells you about how to deal with the way your partner and other female members of your family are going to overrule what you do or say. You may be the househusband, but you are not the mother.

Feeding, changing, cleaning, entertaining the baby, washing and ironing take over your life. Starved of outside stimulation, your brain turns to jelly and you become a brain-dead guppy, who feels dread at the beginning of a new day with the relentless monotony of it all. Your social life falls apart, too, because people no longer find you interesting and invite you to parties. You turn into someone whose brain level has slumped so low that they enjoy watching Dick Van Dyke solve ridiculous TV murder mysteries and find Richard Whiteley a witty and charismatic TV game show host. Yes, life can get that bad.

We can and do get through it, and knowing we all have the same problems (though we deal with them in different ways) may help you to feel better about how you cope with being a father.

Whether you're a seasoned carer or someone who is just thinking about the idea after soft persuasive pillow talk from your partner, you need to know some facts. So come and jump into the househusband swimming pool. It's so deep your feet won't touch the bottom and your armbands will feel like they have holes in them. Take some time out to get a better picture of what you'll be taking on. Grab a chair and a cup of tea, or something stronger, and see what could be in store. But be warned: by the time you've finished reading, you may want to look up the phone number of the clinic to book yourself in for a vasectomy. After all, that discomfort only lasts a few days.

I know that we're all different and, looking back at how I dealt with the problems, there are some things I'd handle differently now. Hindsight is a wonderful thing, but the only way to get it is to have been there. Get the information from people who have walked the walk you are just beginning. I'm not an expert, but at least I've seen through the crap ideas people give out: a lot of it's as much help as a stone park bench is to someone with haemorrhoids.

So get off the bench, grab the haemorrhoid cream and enjoy the rest of the book.

Chapter 1

Countdown to the Birth

No matter who you are, the countdown to the birth of your child is a worrying time. You find yourself reading all the details about the birthing process, and in so much detail that you could work part-time as a midwife.

If you go to antenatal classes, you'll probably be bombarded with videos of women giving birth in all types of positions: in water tanks, on beds, on chairs, on the floor with cushions, on their back, on their front, bent over, bent back or down on all fours. As you watch, you may find yourself thinking: if only the conception could have involved just as many exciting positions. Then, a nurse, with the aid of a rubber band, demonstrates the flexibility of the vaginal opening. She forces the rubber band to what looks like the size of a small dinner plate, to show just how big fully dilated is. Your eyes expand at the same rate as the rubber band, your mouth drops open and your legs cross. Any sexy images you may have had comparing birthing positions to positions of conception disappear, to be replaced by images of John Hurt having convulsions on the table, and then the Alien exploding from his stomach. As the nurse ends her demonstration, you turn to your partner with a loving smile, but you say to yourself, thank God that's not coming out of me!

Just as a point of interest, did you know that it's the male seahorse that gives birth? Isn't nature wonderful, and aren't male seahorses stupid? Out of the billions of life forms on this planet, it's the only one to make that choice.

Most of the information about childbirth is technical and very graphic. At an antenatal class, it's easy to excuse yourself and take refuge in looking for the bathroom to get away from the gore of the evening's talk. But on the big day, things do get graphic, and nine months of waiting build into frantic panic as it gets nearer. For me, looking back and being honest, I must say that the worry of what might go wrong was running through my head so much, that by the time that big day came, I was a mess. Will the baby be all right? Will my wife be OK? And what if something goes wrong at home? Will the car start? Did I lock the front door? Did we pack the hospital bag and the birthing plan?

However, Caroline, my wife, was taking it all in her stride. Apart from her bump getting bigger and her increasing craving for chocolate, she was doing well. It's hard to understand just how much the female body is pushed around inside – with something the size of a football inside her, most of her internal organs were having to fight for space. Her bladder was under so much pressure with all the room the football was taking up, we were going through rolls of toilet paper as if we were a family of six.

Help! My wife's having a baby!

My anxiety about what might go wrong just getting Caroline to the hospital in time kept rising, to the point where every single day I checked the car's tyre pressures, the level of windscreen wash and petrol. (God knows why I found myself checking to see if the light inside the fridge was coming on.) In fact, the North Middlesex Hospital was so close to our house that, if necessary, I could have picked Caroline up and carried her to the delivery room in ten minutes, my adrenalin helping me cope with the extra weight of the unborn baby and Caroline's nine months' chocolate-eating frenzy.

Getting the level of your concern correct for your partner is a bit of a juggling act. If you're too keen to help, you may be accused of fussing too much. If you play it cool, she may take this as a sign that you aren't interested and may whisper in your ear, 'Help me for Christ's sake – it's your baby I'm having. Oh God, get me to the hospital. *Don't* touch me. Don't you know what I'm going through? Men! *Fucking men!*'

Again, around this time, you may be re-thinking any ideas about you being at the birth of your child. I mean, if she's like this now, what's she going to be like when she has to start pushing? You long for the days when a man simply stood in the waiting room handing out cigars and, after being told he was a father, was taken down the pub. But today it's the done thing to have the panicking father hanging around the delivery room feeling as comfortable as a vegetarian in a butcher's shop. Where will it all end? In years to come will family members be invited into the operating theatre, and then tell friends about it over dinner? 'Yes, when Grandfather had his bowel removed, we felt closer as a family. Would you like to see the video of the operation? We sometimes play it backwards.'

When it's your first baby, the not-knowing can take on a life of its own. No matter how much information about childbirth you get your keen little hands on, when the physical bits start to happen, the emotions and stress of the situation help you forget everything. (Apart from the nurse with the rubber band and John Hurt's guts exploding.)

You want help, and flashing away in your brain are your comfort words, 'Hospital, doctor, help! We're having a baby. I'm just a weak, pathetic man and my brain has turned to jelly.' You keep repeating your personal mantra. 'Hospital, doctor, help! My wife's having a baby.' Well, unless you turn into a seahorse on the drive to the hospital, the doctors will know it isn't you who's having the baby.

False Alarm

For us, as for many first-time parents, the first trip to the hospital was a false alarm. But at least it tested my battle plans for getting her there in time, and the plans and I both passed with flying colours: from home to hospital in less than five minutes. It was about 6.30am on a cold December morning. I remember pulling up outside the hospital and starting to open the car door, only to have it wrenched wide by the stormy wind. The rain was horizontal and the hospital entrance offered little protection. No forked lightning, and I didn't see the Four Horsemen of the Apocalypse riding out of the car park, but then, as I said, this was a false alarm.

We'd jumped the gun thinking the baby was coming; but who knows what birth pains feel like if you've never felt them before? If it's your second baby, you know what to expect. If you ever jab yourself with a pin, you don't need to do it again to understand the pain level.

You could say to someone that you've got toothache, but how would you describe that to someone who's never had toothache? Are we talking about a small, jabbing pain, or are we talking about the type of toothache that has you banging your head on the bathroom door? Who's to know what level of pain an individual can control? I mean, you hear stories of women giving birth in the bathroom and claiming after the birth that they didn't know they were pregnant. I may not understand what a woman goes through in giving birth, but I can tell you this: if men had to give birth, the world would be full of one-child families. The worry of a nine-month pregnancy and a few hours of labour, however, are nothing to what you will go through over the next few years with a baby.

OK, back to the hospital with the panicking husband and his calm wife. Entrance, reception and delivery room. We'd been to the hospital before, to get familiar with the surroundings, and I had these areas memorised better than a cabby learning the Knowledge. But when it's happening to you, your best plans fall apart, so we found ourselves at reception, talking to a very relaxed nurse who took down our details. The nurse asked Caroline to go to the bathroom to provide a urine sample, then turned to me and asked, 'How far apart are your wife's contractions, Mr Charlton?'

'Don't know. I've parked my car out the front – will it be all right? Where's my watch?' See what I mean? My brain had turned to jelly. Time for the mantra again: 'Hospital, doctor, help! My wife's having a baby.'

In no time, we found ourselves in a small room with a couple of chairs and a hospital trolley. Caroline was feeling uncomfortable but handling the whole thing very well. I was so pale I wouldn't have looked out of place at a vampires' reunion. The door opened and a doctor walked in and introduced himself, and to this day I can't remember his name. Mind you, with all that was going on, he could have walked in, called me a fat pig and told me my flies were undone, and I'd still have smiled back at him like a brain-dead guppy at feeding time.

After examining her, the doctor told Caroline that she was in the early stages of labour, but that it would still be some time before the birth. I really don't want this to go on much longer, I thought. Can't we get this over with? If I have to go home again and can't have a large whisky to calm myself down because I'm driving, I'll scream.

The doctor said we could stay at the hospital if we liked, but we thought that going back home, to be in a more relaxed atmosphere, would be better. I'm sure it's something the hospital staff see a lot, first-timers thinking the baby's about to shoot out at any minute, only to have the baby announce its rapidly approaching arrival two days later when the mother is in the shopping centre car park.

The real deal

When Caroline and I got home, we laughed about it over a few cups of tea and a few rounds of toast. We were lucky to have such a good hospital on our doorstep, with helpful and understanding staff. With all that had gone on, sleep was the last thing on my mind, but I must have drifted off quickly, as I dreamt about repeating the morning's events.

Just when you thought it was safe to go back to the hospital … You must see the new blockbuster, Alan Returns, Part Five. [Christ, I don't want this to run as long as the Rocky films.] *This time, Alan comes back to the hospital, and he's pissed off. See how he takes control at the reception area. Be amazed as he handles the evil doctor's questioning on contractions. And share in the family's warming joy as our hero holds his newborn son in his arms before he has to save the world from an invasion of giant, killer, clinically depressed seahorses.*

We didn't have to wait long. Within a matter of hours, we were on our way back to the hospital. This time, the hospital and reception area felt more familiar, and Caroline and I were more confident that it was the real deal.

No need for a urine sample this time: straight down to one of the delivery rooms. The hospital staff moved into action, preparing for what, to them, was a common occurrence. Some people want home births, with just a midwife and other members of the family around them. Whatever way you feel is best for you, go for it, but a hospital birth made us feel more comfortable.

People say a hospital birth is a bit like a production line. Well, I suppose it is, but if you live in a city with a few hundred thousand people using the same hospital, what do you expect? If you want to, go to a private clinic, have the delivery room filled with aromatherapy oils, the reflexologist work on your feet, and have your inner spirit calmed by whale song played in your room. If you can afford it, great. But when that baby's head is on its final stretch, you'll feel like kicking the reflexologist off you.

And as for the guy splashing aromatherapy oils and ringing calming bells, you'll want to kick him straight in the bollocks.

Things were moving fast on the Charlton production line by now. Machines bleeping, gas and air pipes hissing and the baby's heartbeat pounding out of a loudspeaker. I felt completely out of my depth, but keeping a lid on the proceedings was our midwife, Amber. Nothing was too much trouble for her, and she gave us fantastic encouragement, support and understanding.

WARNING! If you're currently enjoying a cup of tea and a cheese sandwich, you may need to put them down for a minute. The next bit gets somewhat graphic. My previous understanding of childbirth was, like most men's, based on seeing old films in which the doctor comes downstairs and tells the father to keep out of the way. Doc then tells the maid to get lots of hot water and clean towels. She runs off, crying out, 'Oh Lord! Miss Sarah gonna have her baby.' The next time you see Miss Sarah and the baby, they're cleaned up and rosy-cheeked, with the baby wrapped up in one of the towels and Miss Sarah looking like she's just woken from an afternoon nap.

Think of the film *The Long Good Friday*, the interrogation scene in the abattoir where good old Bob Hoskins has got the guys hanging upside down on meat hooks. Or John Carpenter's film *The Thing*, or any of the *Alien* films. Getting the idea? No? Well, go and buy a large, fresh chicken, cut the string that keeps the legs in place and fill the cavity with tomato ketchup. Now push your hand in and remove the giblets.

Sorry about the above description, but the blood and the mess are a shock, and reading about it doesn't come close to being there – to some degree the father sees more of the messy stuff than the mother does. The best way I can describe how I felt is that it was rather like an out-of-body experience. Standing there, holding Caroline's hand and seeing what was going on, but at the same time taking in the colour of the walls and how many light switches there were in the room.

Amber said, 'The baby's head's coming, Alan. Would you like to see it?' Oh God, I thought, I hope I don't faint and break my nose on that trolley. I remembered hearing stories about fathers who end up in the hospital's emergency department after passing out on the delivery room floor. I was expecting to see something horrible, but hoping to see a rosy-cheeked baby lying in a white towel. What I actually saw was something that looked like a peeled orange covered with ketchup. For some reason, I still felt out of my body – you would think I'd have been more focused on the whole thing. The next few minutes seemed to take forever. I went back and held Caroline's hand, giving her as much encouragement as I could.

'It's a boy!' called Amber. Aaron was born at 10.18am and placed on Caroline's tummy.

'It's a baby!' Caroline called out.

Well, I thought, after all that I bloody well hope so!

Babies aren't born with rosy cheeks: they come out greyish and wrinkled, with bits on, but in the few seconds I spent looking over Aaron and counting his fingers and toes, his little tummy was turning pink. The colour seemed to move across his body in the same way water gets pulled up by blotting paper. The messy bit was not over – the umbilical cord still had to be cut, and the afterbirth still had to be dealt with – but my biggest worry for the past nine months had gone. He looked fine, with everything in the right place.

How the mind drifts at times. I found myself remembering a cartoon I'd seen years ago, I think in *Punch* magazine. In a delivery room, a doctor was looking after a mother who'd just given birth – she looked absolutely exhausted. Standing by her feet was another doctor holding high in the air the most hideous glove puppet you could think of. The concerned doctor was shouting, 'Cut out the jokes Henderson, just show her the baby!'

The cord was cut, and Aaron was taken over to the other side of the delivery room to be checked over and cleaned up.

Without us really noticing, the afterbirth was removed. It looked like a see-through carrier bag filled with chopped liver. Some people want to keep the afterbirth to have it buried, and I remember once reading about some people eating it. Well, the world is a wonderful place and filled with many ideas, and if that's your bag, who am I to judge? But for me, the hospital was welcome to keep it. Maybe I should have taken a look at what was on the hospital's canteen menu for that night.

Caroline had gone through the whole thing without any chemical pain relief. The mix of nitrous oxide and oxygen made her feel sick, so the only pain relief she'd used was a TENS machine, a small box which sends tiny electrical pulses that stimulate the nerves and muscles. She could control the level of power to help her with the pain, which for me was great because throughout the whole thing she didn't shout at me once.

Now what do we do?

Once the checks were done, Aaron was given back to us, and we were left on our own to take in the whole range of emotions that we had just been through. Like any new father I thought he was absolutely beautiful, but this wasn't what I would call a bonding experience – for me that didn't happen for some time. I was just pleased it was over and everything had gone well. After a little while, there was a knock on the door and in walked Amber with a big smile on her face. I'm sure seeing one of 'her' mothers with a new baby must make her job feel very special. Amber told us it was time for Caroline and Aaron to be taken up to the ward.

It was also time for me to make some phone calls and fetch some things from home. I felt a bit bad about leaving them both, and maybe I did fuss just a little bit too much before going. Getting the feeling from Caroline that she wanted to sleep for a week, I kissed my family goodbye and said I'd be back soon.

Caroline and Aaron stayed in the hospital for the next three days, with me visiting them three times a day, bringing messages, cards and food parcels. Wasn't Loyd Grossman going to do something about hospital food? God knows what he'd have come up with for the mothers on the maternity ward. 'Your main course for tonight, ladies, is your afterbirth, marinated in red wine and garlic, flame-grilled and served on a bed of fresh lettuce.'

The ward Caroline and Aaron were on had six beds. You couldn't call it restful, what with visitors calling in and six babies crying at any time of the day or night, but you did have the comfort of knowing that help was just the push of a button away.

You soon get down to basics with a baby with just the acts of feeding and changing them. I remember going in one afternoon and finding Caroline changing Aaron's nappy. Now, if you don't know this, a newborn baby's poo is made on another planet. It sticks to the baby's body like Velcro. Feeling about as confident as someone diving off the high board for the first time, we tried to clean this alien excrement off our son, but the more uptight we got, the more Aaron screamed.

Then we heard a cry of 'Oh my little darling, what are your mother and father doing to you?'

A nurse with the appearance and bubbly personality of Rusty Lee picked Aaron up and carried him over to the washing area. She laid him face down along the inside of her arm, her hand holding him firmly and safely, and she washed his little bum under warm running water. Aaron stopped crying and his face showed his confidence in the person who'd taken control and stopped the mess Mum and Dad were making of cleaning him up. The nurse brought him back to us and with a big smile said, 'Here we go, clean and happy and back to Mummy. It's OK. You won't break him, you know.'

Two things I got from this were: 1. Babies pick up on the confidence of the person holding them. 2. If I didn't get the hang of this bum-cleaning thing, the Charlton family's overuse of paper towels would wipe out the rest of the rainforest.

Chapter 2

 ## On Your Own in the Deep End, and Dealing with It

Caroline and Aaron were coming home the next day, so it was time to clean up the house and get everything ready. The house looked and smelt like a group of students had been staying for a few weeks: coffee cups and glasses tucked out of sight under papers and old socks, takeaway meal cartons all over the place…

How could a place fall apart in just three days? So, on went the music (loud) and the Hoover: the clean-up mission had started. I was making good progress with the cleaning, but decided to leave the rest for when I got back from the last evening visit to the hospital.

They both looked great. I gave Caroline her food parcel and played goo-goo-ga-ga with Aaron. I think he was impressed with his father's mastery of this game in such a short time. Caroline was keen to get home, so was looking forward to the next day, but we were both a little bit frightened and apprehensive about having to cope with a newborn baby.

When I got home, I finished the cleaning and put out all the flowers that friends and family had sent us. I poured a large whisky and sat down to relax. I remember considering just how much money florists must make from the baby business. (With hindsight, I should have treasured that night a lot more: it was the last peaceful night's sleep I was to have for about ten years.)

As this book is mainly a guide for full-time fathers, I'm sure you won't mind me putting down some of the ground rules for the guys. Your role as the one who looks after the baby has not started yet. People will have no interest at all in what you have to say about your baby. Don't worry. This is normal for us fathers and in time you'll learn to deal with it. Over the years, nature and society have moulded society's view of motherhood and of who looks after the baby to such a degree that you, the father, have about as much chance of being heard as a drowning man's cry for help in the middle of the Atlantic Ocean. But look on the bright side. You won't be missed in a room full of people until one of the guests needs their drink topped up. No need to put on clean clothes or shave, for that matter – who's going to notice? When the baby's mother is in the room, you are not needed and not noticed by others.

Just me and you, kid

Now, depending on the arrangements you've made with work about when you'll stop (and when your wife or partner goes back to work), you'll have your countdown to your first full day on your own with the baby. It comes round quickly, so make good use of the lead-up time. Get to grips with the basics now. For example, if your partner's breastfeeding, that's great, but you'll still have to sterilise the bottles you need to feed the baby. The way a baby feeds from its mother is different from the way it feeds from a bottle, which only puts more shit on your shovel when your partner's at work and feeding the baby is your problem. Technology's a wonderful thing, but all the phone calls, e-mails, faxes and web links in the world won't get that comforting breast and its milk locked onto your baby's mouth. Breast may be best, but nature hasn't caught up with us men on this yet, so get used to cleaning and preparing those bottles.

One problem with breastfeeding is that when your partner comes home the baby can smell that walking milk bank. If your partner lets the baby lock onto the breast milk when she walks through the door, you're back to square one. The baby's going to get pretty pissed off the next morning when you try to ram a plastic bottle into its mouth. I mean, which would you prefer to cuddle up with? No matter how many ice trays you fill with breast milk, or how many times you warm it up in a bottle, the baby knows it's not the same.

From caveman to seahorse

For most people in the world and from as far back as when man started to walk on two legs, the female has been the one who cared for the baby. Men went out, caught and killed the dinner and dragged it back to the family cave. Back then, roles were on a more basic level and, apart from the poor old seahorse, that was the way the world grew.

A few hundred thousand years later, things have changed. Wars, crime, work, radio, television, mortgage payments, workers' rights, civil rights, animal rights, interest rates, education, videos, CDs, DVDs and blue-tinted contact lenses. We're bombarded daily with images of who or what we should be, from caring for the poor souls who, through no fault of their own, face death from famine, to paying the rent, buying that new car or the latest mobile phone, or getting that perfect body and whiter teeth. We can choose how much we want to get involved with the rat race, and sometimes just looking at the news can put your own problems into perspective, but the mother is still the one who has, wants and controls the babies – and hence the population.

And then, after a few thousand years and with all the shit that's going on in the world, we stand up as a new form of animal and say, 'Look, we are househusbands.' How much support do we think we'll get from the rest of the world? Let me tell you: fuck all. Other men see us as a joke and if you fill out a form asking your occupation, you have to tick the 'Unemployed' box. I don't want a debate about it; I'm just saying, you'll have to deal with attitudes that are locked tighter than a submarine hatch.

I'm not talking about people who through the loss of a loved one or through separation have found themselves the main carer. Being a househusband through choice is still rare and we still aren't seen as a large part of the fabric of society.

When men come home from work, they may see and play with their children in the evening, read them bedtime stories and kiss them goodnight. And the male partner is often used as a threat with older children: 'Just wait till your father gets home.' Fathers see the role the mother has and hopefully respect that role. Inside they know that much more input might cause problems between them and their partner. OK, we may be going back over old ground, repeating that women have been looking after babies and bringing up children longer than men have. The point I'm getting at is that in the workplace a woman can be as cold and ruthless as any man, but when she comes home she may instinctively take on the traditionally female role as the main carer. This can push you out of the role that's been yours all day and can make you feel undermined. Like some of her male colleagues, she may not even give a toss about the problems her partner's had at home all day.

Whoever's at home looking after the baby may fall into the same trap. You're working in the family home and your partner may not see it as 'real work'. This takes time – maybe years – to work through, but eventually cracks appear. How you cope with these cracks is up to you. You've been open-minded in giving up your paying job to support your partner's career by bringing up the children, but, in time, what you did no longer carries any weight, and your partner and people outside grow to feel that you're 'just at home' and your partner's the one who's 'really' working. Deep down, most men know they don't want to cope with caring for the children and most are pig-ignorant about what's involved. So, as seahorses – sorry, househusbands – we know we're taking on something most men have the good sense not to.

OK ladies, how many of you are thinking: God, this guy's a real wimp, moaning on about how hard looking after a baby and bringing up children can be? Yes, you're right, I am a wimp. It's the hardest thing I have had to do and put up with in my life so far. You're justified in calling me a wimp if you yourself have had children and have felt the depression, frustration and stress that aren't openly talked about when it comes to staying at home looking after a baby. But as a woman you get more back-up than men do. You can get together with other mums having the same problems, at coffee mornings, mothering groups and so on. Just while wheeling the pram down to the shops, a mother will get supportive comments from other mothers. When people see a guy out with the baby, they think that the mother must be sick at home or that he's separated from the mother and this is his allotted day out.

So, guys, you'll feel very much on your own, thrown in the deep end, and you'll have to deal with problems you wouldn't have dreamed of as being problems before. But, like I said at the beginning, it does help to know that others have felt the same way. There are a number of times in any man's life when he feels out of his depth as regards events going on around him. Your partner giving birth is one of those events, and, because you're a man, you feel thoroughly out of place. Even though it was one of the biggest things I've been partly responsible for, at times I was at a loss as to what to do or say.

Look, I know I've started off with all guns blazing and I may come over as a miserable bastard [Note from author's wife: You are!], and the choice you have made or are about to make about staying at home is yours. But I want to tell it as it is – or, should I say, as I've found it to be. I'll try as best I can to describe some of the most wonderful feelings you can ever have, such as when your child falls asleep on your lap or comes to you for comfort. You'll have more of these joyful moments than most men, precisely because you're the one who's there with the children. This joy will be one of the hardest things to get across to you if you've never felt it, but you're lucky to have the chance to experience it.

But you do pay a price. For my part, I had years of feeling depressed. No one helped me, and why should they have? We all lie about how we are coping. And my self-loathing hit rock-bottom and took away some of the happy feelings I should have had with my children. I felt I was doing things wrong. It's easy to doubt yourself when you're surrounded with images from the TV and the press about how wonderful it all is. I know now that everyone, male or female, who looks after children goes through this. I know as a man that the feelings hit us on a different level, and talking to other househusbands supports this. We're all different and we'll all feel out of our depth and on different levels. I hope you are having, or will have, a wonderful time bringing up your children, and there are many out there who've coped well and enjoyed the whole thing more than I have. But if one day you find yourself slamming a door with frustration, or find yourself screaming at invisible people in your house, or have cried because you feel at rock-bottom, don't forget that others have been there too. As I said, that knowledge can help you cope and enjoy the good bits more, and help you find your own way of dealing with the bad bits.

So, I hope you've got this far without too many interruptions? I promise you there are some happier bits coming up. Take a break, see if the washing machine's finished, and stop the baby putting biscuits in the video machine. When you next have a few minutes to spare, I'll see you in Chapter 3.

Chapter 3

Getting to Grips: Feeding and Changing

Hi guys. Good to have you back. I'll write quietly so we don't wake the baby. Depending on your lifestyle and on how much you and your partner each put into chores like cleaning before you had the baby, your share of free time will change a lot. From now on you'll learn a lot about housework, for a start. Your practical skills will take off like a rocket; you have a whole New World to explore, a New World of understanding things like what a sink is for. And then there's something you've seen but never before turned on: a washing machine. Along with this comes a washing line and a whole new relationship with something called an 'iron'.

In fact, you'll find the iron no longer gets put away in the cupboard because it's used so often. It now spends more time in the front room or on the kitchen worktop than in the cupboard. What's the point of packing it away when you'll need it again so soon? I would say that in many homes with children the iron and ironing board take on the role of a piece of furniture. Standing ready for action in the front room, taking the overspill of magazines and coffee cups, but always ready to be plugged in.

You're probably laughing to yourself, and you may be put out because you feel I'm being a little patronising. That's because you're thinking about things as they used to be – you know, when you were cleaning just for yourself. One plate and a couple of cups to wash up, and you only met the iron once a week. As for the ironing of baby clothes, you may be thinking that baby clothes are small and, if it's a large iron, just one press and the job's done. True enough, but a baby can get through three to five changes of clothes a day. That's around thirty-five items a week, 140 a month or 1,680 in the first year – add your own and your partner's clothes to the pile and you can see why you have to start allowing more time for jobs that used to take no time at all.

Now get your head round this: not only do you have to add time to the jobs you did easily before, but you have to distort time as well. Say it used to take you two minutes to iron a shirt when all the time in the world was yours and the only thing that might disturb those two minutes was the need to scratch your arse or pick your nose. With a baby, before the iron has even warmed up, you're needed. What with giving them a different toy to play with or changing their nappy, we have to add between five and ten minutes to that two-minute job. And the great thing is the baby can repeat this trick many times. Now add some other things that can disturb the baby and make them want you. Things like the phone ringing, the doorbell, next door's loud music, traffic, car horns, wind blowing, trees growing, flies flying, bees buzzing or even ants bonking in the back garden. Or, to put it into househusband terms, it can take all goddam day to iron one fucking shirt.

And don't go getting any bright ideas about doing the

ironing when the baby is asleep during the day – if you do, you're not thinking yet from the practical part of your brain or as someone who's looking after a baby. OK, you could iron when the baby's asleep, but as you've had only four hours' sleep in the past twenty-four, don't you think you might just take a thirty-minute nap in your chair with your baby?

Anyway, with a little bit of arranging, the extra jobs can be fitted in. It depends a bit on your partner, but extra time can be found in the evenings and on weekends. You know, evenings, the time when before you would have gone to a club, seen a film, had a drink and curry with your friends. Weekends, when before you'd have gone to football or checked out the new cars in the showroom, or lain in bed on a Sunday morning with your partner. You see, part of the joy of having a baby is that they show you just how much time you used to waste.

So, guys, get used to this distorted time idea as soon as you can. You can get the work done – the only thing you have to accept is that your life has been put on hold. If you have your baby when you're thirty, you'll next find yourself with a bit of time to do things you like when you're forty-one. Yep, that time-distortion thing just creeps up on you. And please believe me when I tell you that the joy you felt at your football team winning a match or after the best night out you had with your mates is nothing compared to the first time your baby sleeps right through the night and you actually get six hours' unbroken sleep.

Babies work on a different time line from adults. The idea of night being the time to close your eyes and sleep is one which all adults understand, but babies take some years to get to grips with it. In the meantime, Baby works according to its own ideas, waking up at, say, 10.45pm, back to sleep at 12.15am, awake again from 1.45am to around 4.45am. I've found myself ironing at 11pm – quite enjoyable with a late film and a beer, but then I've been doing this job for a long time. Like grabbing at straws, househusbands have to take any moment that's quiet and call it fun. To read about disrupted sleep on the page is as easy as reading the page number, but in fact the fatigue and stress this sleep pattern builds up are cancerous to any relationship.

Feeding time at the zoo

So you can see that househusbands have to become good time-managers. They also have to become very good at doing several things at once. One of the most important times of the day is feeding time. In the early days all you have to deal with is bottle-feeding and, at first, it's a nerve-racking idea. From how you hold the baby to what type of bottle and teat you use, I never thought that so much effort was required just to feed a baby.

Before I took over full-time with Aaron, Caroline breast-fed. Like many mothers, she didn't always find it easy and as I was to be the one taking over in a few weeks, the three of us had the frustrating task of trying to work the two very different ways of getting milk into Aaron. All a baby has to do is cry its displeasure and the parents run around like headless chickens. So the house can become a farmyard with the baby screaming like a piglet in a sty, while Mum and Dad cluck frantically at each other like chickens surprised by a fox.

'Cluck cluck, did you warm the milk?'

'Yes, cluck.'

'Cluck, did you put the right amount of milk formula in the bottle?'

'Yes, cluck.'

'*Cluck,* the teat – did you put the right teat on the bottle?'

'*Yes,* cluck cluck fucking cluck!'

Choosing the milk formula with so many on the market is a puzzle, and then there's the type of bottle and the size of the teat. Add the many ways of cleaning and sterilising and making up a feed is a lesson in chemistry and stress management.

Sterilising bottles is important and I never got on with the ones that did not use some form of electricity. For me the best steriliser is one that holds about four bottles and all the bits. It looks a bit like a round, see-through plastic cake tin to which you add a very small amount of tap water. You then cook the whole thing in the microwave for a couple of minutes, after which the cleaned bottles are ready to go.

If you haven't started your caring full-time, this will all be new to you. Have you ever thought how much effort goes into getting a bottle of milk down a baby? The way babies become attached to one type of bottle is amazing. I suppose it's the same as an adult staying with the same toothpaste, men liking the same style of razor and women using the same kind of conditioner. Other products may do the same job but they don't feel the same. I remember once trying to feed Aaron with a different bottle, and he wouldn't have it. Actually, it wasn't so much the bottle as a different-shaped teat that was the problem. He was hungry and wanted the milk, but Daddy had put a different teat on the bottle and he was going to make me pay. Patience and logic are two of the things that disappear from a person who's just started looking after a baby. Being locked in a house with a crying baby who won't take his feed is very stressful. Even a puppy will eat food from an unfamiliar bowl or plate.

Aaron's crying forced me out the house. I put him in the pushchair, which wasn't easy as he was wriggling all over the place. It would have been easier to wrestle, kill and make a pair of boots out of a crocodile than strap him into his pushchair. It took me quite some time to get out of the house. At one point I thought I'd had a brain haemorrhage but then realised I'd simply head-butted the doorframe a bit too hard. Still, it helped relieve some stress. About ten minutes from our house there's a chemist's. The walk and the pushchair calmed Aaron down a bit, but he started up again when we went into the shop. Guys, when you're out with your baby and the baby's crying, people always look at you, tut and make comments about you and the baby to their friends. To avoid too many comments, I found, grabbed and paid for the replacement teat and was out of the shop before the till drawer was shut.

On the way back I talked to Aaron, telling him that Daddy had just got him a new teat and that when we got home he could have his bottle. Aaron looked at me with about as much interest as a puppy has in the type of bowl its food is served in. By the time we walked through the door he had had enough rest in the pushchair to bring his crying back to full volume. I ripped open the packet, washed the teat under the tap, put it on the bottle and put it in Aaron's mouth, without even taking him out of the pushchair. The whole episode, starting with the walk to the chemist and ending with Aaron happy with the teat and downing the bottle, took around thirty minutes. To me it felt like hours and I was physically drained by it.

Logic says that if I'd cleaned and sterilised one of the old bottles sitting by the kitchen sink, peace, joy and harmony would have come to the Charlton household in about five minutes. You may think you'd have done the sensible thing and cleaned one of the other bottles and teats and used them. Yes, that would have been best. But with the smallest thing driving us to the brink of insanity, we've all done things and thought afterwards that we should have done them differently.

Once, I opened a bottle of medicine and the cardboard disc that you sometimes get in the plastic bottle-cap dropped on the kitchen floor. Still with the cap in my right hand and the bottle in my left, I went to pick it up. As sure as fresh buttered toast will always land on the floor butter-side down, the sticky ring left on the disc by the medicine had glued it to the tiled kitchen floor, and my short-nailed chubby fingers couldn't get it off. If I'd put the cap down, I'd have got a better hold on the disc, but that would have meant being logical about the problem. Instead, I found myself using a method many men use. I shouted at it. 'You effing bastard! Come on, you bastard!' You may be thinking of all the ways I could have got the disc off the floor, from sweeping it up with a dustpan and brush to sliding a knife under the edge of the disc and flipping it over. No. My next idea was to stamp on it. 'If I can't pick you up, I'll destroy you, you bastard! Why do they put a paper disc inside the bottle-cap anyway?' I shouted at an empty kitchen. At this point, my attention was drawn to my left hand, which was covered in medicine and still holding the by-now empty bottle. Bottle and cap went in the bin, and I spent the next fifteen minutes cleaning up the mess. With the kitchen looking cleaner and the paper disc still glued to the floor, but now armed with a practical plan, I went and bought a new bottle of medicine.

I'm sure you've done something like that: found yourself running around like a headless chicken and heading up the wrong path completely. With the bottle and the teat, I saw the new teat as the problem and felt I had to get a new one of the kind Aaron was happy with. There may have been some logic in my madness, but it sent me up the wrong path with no speed limit and blindfolded by my madness.

In time, your saviour does come, in the form of getting a routine. As we're all so different, what suits one person may not work for someone else. The best way to feed your baby will be what works best for you. Most days, you're pleased just to make it to the end of the day; it takes about six to eight months to get to grips with the whole thing. Give yourself time to cope. Remember learning to drive and how impossible it seemed at first that you'd ever master the car? It takes an average of one driving lesson for every year of your age to pass a driving test, but a baby won't stop doing something when you press a pedal, or move when you press another. At first the jobs that need doing most often – such as making up a bottle-feed or changing a nappy – can take forever.

When you prepare a bottle-feed, you have to measure out so many fluid ounces of water and pour the cooled-down boiled water into the bottle, exactly up to the line. Then you add so many level spoonfuls of milk powder, using the plastic spoon that comes with the tin. Your measurements are finer than a diamond-cutter's, but as the months go by you can do the job much faster. With a confident flick, you knock the excess powder off the measuring spoon, add water that has cooled down from when you made your last cup of coffee and shake the baby-milk cocktail with the confidence of a top-class barman.

I once overheated Aaron's feed and, as I shook the bottle to mix the powder and water, I discovered that, with very hot water, the pressure in a bottle on the kitchen table is great enough to force the milk out of the teat with the power of a jet wash and for it to hit the kitchen ceiling. If this happens when you're a beginner, you can panic, sending the stream of pressurised milk all over the kitchen. You've lost most of the milk, so you start again with a fresh bottle. In time this mistake will probably happen again. Don't panic, just think about a new colour for the kitchen ceiling. As the years go by, many parents become such experts in bottle temperature that they can angle the milk jet into the sink, undo the top, flick in a little more powder, and add cold water by bunging it under the tap.

That reminds me of a television ad many years ago with Arthur Mullard. Arthur was a large man with a deep, gravelly voice and a face that looked like it had been round the boxing ring a few times. In films and on TV he always played the slow-minded thug. Anyway, the ad was set in a London street and Arthur, who was working in a roadside mobile café, served a well-dressed man a cup of coffee. On trying the coffee, the man said, 'Oh dear, this coffee is strong and bitter. I don't want this.'

Leaning over him, Arthur replied, 'Shall I bung it under the tap?'

'Oh no. Adding water will just take away the aroma and flavour of the coffee.'

Looking very threatening, Arthur said, 'I know what you want. You want that new Mellow Birds coffee that has the full ground flavour and aroma of fresh coffee but without that strong, bitter taste.'

'Oh yes. Do you have some?'

Arthur replied, 'No. Shall I bung it under the tap?'

I don't know why I remember that ad, apart from it being funny, but sometimes the answer to a problem is simple, such as my half-hour of stress over getting a new teat, when I should have just bunged one of the old ones under the tap.

When you're looking after children, there are times that mark a big change in your routine. The first is when you no longer have to sterilise the baby bottles and anything else you feed your baby with. The steriliser is an old friend, but also one you are pleased to see the back of. Getting used to finding it easy to make up a feed in a bottle that has just been washed in the sink is great. Other such times are having your baby out of nappies or when they can hold their bottle or feed themselves.

... and straight out the other end!

So much for getting to grips with bottle-feeding. But I'm sure you've been thinking about that other problem we have to face: the one involving your baby's understanding of Newton's Third Law of Motion, the one that says every action has an equal and opposite reaction. Not with a baby, it hasn't. You feed in six ounces of milk in one end and you get six pounds of soft mess the other end. What goes in white, warm and smelling sickly sweet comes out hot, black and pungent. Yes, guys, I'm talking about nappy-changing. Your cute little bundle of joy can give you a present which can have you retching even before you've released the nappy tabs and viewed the contents full on.

As I said earlier, the first time Caroline and I changed Aaron's nappy we made a pig's ear of the whole thing. When we got home, the problem with changing the nappy was a shared thing, and we helped and encouraged each other. I clearly remember the first time I changed a nappy on my own. The walk upstairs to do the job had the speed and eagerness of someone going to the dentist. But it was something I was going to have to get used to and I had to start sometime.

I'd started to sweat before I even laid Aaron on the changing mat. I did everything wrong. I took off the nappy before I'd got the new one ready and, worse still, the cleaning wipes were still in the box.

A quick comment on getting wipes out: you pull them out of the box in the same way you pull a paper hankie out of its box to blow your nose or to catch a sneeze. The one you pull out brings the corner of the next one out, ready to use. It's a great idea and works well – until, that is, you need one in a hurry, and then the wipe will be stuck to the box more firmly than a paper disc to the kitchen floor.

You may come to refer to nappy changes as two- or three-wipe jobs, that being the number of wipes it takes to clean up the mess. After months of practice you will get the job under your belt and can judge the number of wipes just by the weight and smell of the nappy. But Baby will keep you on your toes with the odd eight- or even ten-wipe delivery.

Back to my first effort: the sweat was now dripping off my nose and I was locked into the job. I got the nappy undone and took hold of Aaron's legs, lifting his bum off the changing-mat. The first wipe went to work and cleaned off most with the first attack, but with the smearing came a release of strong gases. I was hit with the smell of pickled onions and of a bottle of milk that had been left out of the fridge for a week. I know I was new to the game, but I'd never give a newborn baby pickled onions to eat. Was Aaron climbing out of his cot at night and raiding the kitchen cupboard? The answer to the question of how a baby feeding only on breast milk could smell of pickled onions was that it came from the milk. It's true, guys. What the mother eats can be transferred into her milk, and Caroline had eaten pickled onions the night before. Well, I thought, from now on she can drink perfume and eat oranges.

Locked in the bathroom, I lost all sense of time, feeling sure I'd missed my birthday (which wasn't for another nine months – from the time I went into the bathroom, anyway). Once I got the filled nappy into the scented nappy sack, I could breathe again. Aaron lay still, with a strange look on his face. Maybe he didn't like the smell – I mean he was nearer to it than I was. The new nappy went on OK. Well, the second new nappy went on OK. For some reason, on the first one the sticky tabs that hold the nappy together had no stick on them. Maybe some joker at the factory thought it amusing not to put glue on a few nappies and in the pub that night he'd laughed with his mates about it over a beer, just like in the scary old story about the guy in a condom factory with a pin.

Eventually, having washed and changed, I opened the bathroom door and gave the clean-smelling baby back to Caroline, who looked pleased that the job was done but concerned at my appearance. The next few minutes I spent cleaning up the bathroom and opening a window to get rid of the smell. You do get used to the smell, along with developing the technique of breathing through your mouth so that as little as possible goes up your nose.

I know the smell's natural but there's no need to inflict it on anyone else. So why don't people use the bathroom to change their baby, especially when they have guests or when they go to someone else's house? No, they plonk Baby down on the floor in the middle of a room full of people and change the nappy. That's fine when you're on your own in the house, but why do some feel it's OK to invite everyone else in the room to view and smell what their baby's done? I mean, if you were at a dinner party would you lift your left cheek off the chair and fart as the hostess brought in the main course? Would you piss over the tablecloth as the brandy and coffees were served?

Anyway, my first single-handed nappy change was over. It had taken about fifteen minutes, and I'd lost four pounds in sweat. It took some time and several cups of tea before I felt myself again, and it was a long time before I could do the job like a professional.

Over the next few years I repeated this feeding, changing and cleaning routine many times a day: cleaning, wiping and mopping up mess, catching a handful of vomit that Aaron brought up after a feed. The house smelt of nappies, vomit and disinfectant, and if Aaron had a cold my T-shirts looked as if I'd been run over by a large snail. I found myself only shaving at the weekend because, while brushing my teeth with Aaron in one arm was safe enough, just picture trying to shave holding a crying baby. The free time to use the toilet disappeared – having to take a baby in with you can put you off, but then so can the baby screaming outside as you try to pee. It does put you off, doesn't it, guys? You know that feeling – when you're standing at a row of empty urinals and some guy walks in and stands at the one next to you. Apart from it stopping you in mid-flow, you think: what the hell does he want? The flow of relief doesn't come back until he's gone.

When your partner comes home in the evening, you can have the toilet to yourself again. But if nature's being tough on you and you need to have a crap during the day, what do you do with the baby? Lay him on the floor outside the bathroom with the door open so you can still call to him and say goo-goo to keep him happy? What if you put him down and he's screaming and your stomach's burning with the need to go? Well, sitting on the toilet and holding a baby to stop it crying has you thinking about your role in life, I can tell you. If you take advantage of nappy-changing time to use the toilet, don't make the mistake of leaving the new nappy off. If the baby's a boy, not only will he use that time to poo on the changing-mat, but his bladder can give enough water pressure to shower your feet as you sit on the toilet – besides spraying himself and the rest of the bathroom – so after you finish on the toilet, you find yourself on all fours cleaning up the mess. You may start thinking, 'How much would it cost to get a live-in nanny? Is it a rollover on the lottery this week?'

We've all heard about the cost of bringing up a baby. It can run into thousands of pounds a year, not least because there's the loss of your salary if you stay at home or the cost of child-care if you work. Put it this way: if Chris Tarrant offered you the same amount on *Who Wants to Be a Millionaire?* you'd think your dreams had come true and would feel set up for life. So we all have to swallow the 'children cost a lot of money' pill. You can't always see the money going. It hides itself in places and things you can't remember buying. The big things, like pushchair, cot, high chair and car seat, all have an 'I can see it' value. It's the little, but still important, things that add up, like extra washing powder and washing-up liquid, tissues and kitchen paper towels, all of which you use in greatly increased quantities. Your washing machine has for years happily done your weekly wash, but now, having to cope with a daily attack, it may give up under the increased workload. The washing machine companies must rub their hands with glee with every new baby they see. So now you know why, when you walk into a shop with your partner and baby, the salesman is so pleased to help you. You're a walking wallet and the baby is happily giving the salesman permission to take your wallet straight from your back pocket. Yes, when you add children to your partnership, you'll be looking at more bills than you'd see on a large duck pond. Look guys, I'd better get going. I have to do the school run; we can cover the money thing a bit more later on. So put the kettle on or warm up that iron, and I'll see you later.

Chapter 4

Rules of the House

This chapter is going to make you feel as though you're stuck in the middle of a minefield and you can't see where it starts or where it ends. You know that the mines are set two feet apart, but you haven't yet grasped the fact that it's not only standing on one that can blow you to bits – these mines are also triggered by a wrong word, a missed feed, the time of the month, time of the week, making a cup of coffee or not making a cup of coffee.

You may be thinking, why is a book that claims to be a survival guide for fathers comparing the rules of the house to standing in a minefield? Well, I'm not talking about rules in the way you're used to. Luckily, most of the ones you follow in your day-to-day life are set, and you know and work around them every day. House rules with a baby are different and they change. This knowledge will help you to survive. Let me give you an example. We all know that when driving a car, we follow rules. If we come to a red traffic light, we stop. That's a rule all motorists understand, and everyone is happy about it. Let's turn that simple rule round, using the adjustments that only having a baby can make. Say that the red-light rule was changed one morning, so that red was Go and green was Stop, and the only warning of the change was a thirty-second news report on breakfast-time radio. How relaxing would your journey to work be that morning? Now we add the next step, which is that the rule gets changed back to red meaning Stop, but only on Mondays and Fridays. On Tuesdays and Sundays, all the lights are turned off and you have to get permission from the driver on your right before you can cross at a junction. After a month of this, would you still be driving? Or would you take up embroidery, or maybe start making your own pillows, stuffed with the hair you pulled out while driving over the past month?

If you're new to this baby thing, my example may seem a little over the top. You may feel the author is sitting in a padded room from which all sharp objects have been removed, and is writing on lined paper using wax crayon, with dribble coming from the side of his mouth. Well, you can make your final decision about the state of my mind when you get to the end of the book, but read on and just see how mad 'mad' can get.

Who's the daddy?

A big problem you'll have once you take over full-time care is, now that your partner's back at work, deciding who lays down the rules. It's necessary to have some rules of the house, but be careful and tread softly. Setting rules before you had a baby was easy. Who's making dinner, cleaning the house, and what shall we do at the weekend? Piece of cake. No mines going off in this relationship and if they did, you could always walk out the door and find someone new. But one thing your new little ray of sunshine brings into your relationship is a switch and it's big enough to switch on any size of minefield. Before, you'd have come to a compromise with your partner: 'This weekend we'll go to the theatre, but next week we'll go and see the film, OK?' Both of you are happy bunnies who still talk to each other. Babies will take away any compromises and will have you just giving in. Remember, you're a househusband in name only. By the time society recognises your role, the human race will be fighting the Klingon Empire and we'll be beaming all over the place.

Giving in is something the person who looks after the baby does a lot. I did and I don't recommend it. Having to control others' input to your ideas will have you stepping on mines. I made a lot of rods for my own back, which left me angry and frustrated with friends and family, over things ranging from trying to get a sleeping routine for Aaron to feeling I wanted to kill his grandparents because they gave him a chocolate biscuit when I'd asked them not to. Boom! See what I mean? Not only are you stepping on mines, but now the grandparents are throwing grenades at you.

You will make a rod for your back every day if you give in over many of the things that frustrate you, and when people break the rules you've set, bombs are likely to go off. You can either put up with it or else deal with it out in the open. Only you can judge which is better for you, as only you know your partner and how willing she is to compromise. But once you have a baby, you'll both change, so what at one time would have been an easy problem to deal with will become much more serious if you don't talk it through. Add to the mixture your fears about looking after a baby. Because neither of you has ever had these feelings before and both of you are new to the experience, your frustrations can pour out. Not being able to understand or talk about them will have you taking your frustrations out on each other. Other people may well see you as a grumpy bastard, someone who doesn't want help, who is self-centred and single-minded.

I'm not going to tell you how to get help or ideas from other people about how best to deal with a situation – there are too many and we are all different – nor set out a step-by-step guide. Most people who have a family just get through it day-by-day, looking forward to the time when they won't have to deal with that problem again. Many of us end up brain-dead like that. We just go through the motions, because at the time it's easier and you just want to keep the peace in the family.

Sticking by the rules of your house will be harder than it is for an addict to come off heroin. Why? Family and loved ones want the addict to come off the drug, because they know the addiction will kill. People overlook the idea that the househusband may feel suicidal with the frustration of not being taken seriously over matters of child-care. Without support from the people closest to him, the feeling can get out of hand very quickly. Years of a miserable existence for the househusband can follow, leaving him unable to enjoy some of the best times he'll ever have with his children. He's eaten up by resentment of the decision for him to stay at home and look after the children, with no possibility of getting work until the child's at school. OK, I know I've jumped the gun and a few years by talking about the kids being at school, but you find yourself looking forward to a future when things get easier, and when the kids start nursery or playschool you do feel better.

The freedom you feel when your baby is out of nappies is great, and when they can use the toilet by themselves that's another big step. But steps like those are separated by years and, in between, your depression has each day to work on you. I'm being as upfront as I can. We all get the looking-after bit wrong from time to time, but as someone with eleven years' experience as a househusband I tell you this: every time you let your partner break a rule regarding your rights as the main carer, you feel less able or willing to carry on. Women looking after their children have had all this, and for some reason their hormones still tell them to go through it again and have more children: I can respect many of the problems women go through when looking after the baby and taking care of the home, but as a man, evolution still has some catching up to do with us on this full-time child-care thing.

But evolution is slow. I know sometimes there's the odd bang of speed like the dinosaurs dying out, but that was an asteroid hitting the Earth, wasn't it? Hang on, I've just had an idea. Let me get some more crayons and wipe the corners of my mouth and I'll tell you about it.

The dinosaurs died out suddenly after millions of years of happily going about the job of just being a dinosaur. Who knows why it happened? Scientists tell us an asteroid hit the Earth and suddenly that was the end. But what if the idea of sexual equality came to the female dinosaurs and the male dinosaurs had to take on more of a caring role? Dinosaurs were big and powerful but they had a brain the size of a peanut. Maybe the shock of the twenty-first-century idea that the male should look after the baby dinosaurs was too much for his brain to deal with. It must have been devastating when, suddenly, the male dinosaur was looking after the baby *T-rex*. I mean, be late with that bottle-feed and the baby would bite your leg off. No chemists, so no teething gel, Calpol or anti-depressants available, and the pub and off-licence won't be around for a few million years. With no sleep and a lousy sex life, no wonder they died out. Before they had the idea of the male staying at home, at least they'd been around for a few million years. Man's had only a few thousand years, so as a new life form, how much more time do househusbands have?

What's upsetting you at the moment, I don't know. You may be a more strong-minded person than I am. What's more, I'm sure there's another househusband somewhere in the country writing about how wonderful the whole thing has been, how much closer he feels to his children, how he got so much joy from the experience and, yes, the sun shone every day and the birds sang. Let me suggest a title for that book: *Ignoring the Elephant's Bollocks*.

Dad knows best

The initial rules you have to set may at first seem easy. They revolve around feeding and changing the baby and, hopefully, getting them to sleep at a time your body clock fully agrees with. If you find a way of feeding that works and keeps the baby happy, stick with it. You can make that a rule and later add all the other parts of the feeding rule, such as how you like to clean the bottle, what size teat you want, or whether you mix the milk powder into the water or add the water to the powder then pour the mix into the bottle. This may seem over the top and petty and, yes, as I write it, it does sound off the wall. But if your partner's driven you up the wall in the past by leaving the top off the toothpaste, leaving the toilet seat up (or down) or by farting in bed, changing the way you've been doing something with the baby will have you climbing the walls so often your fingernails will bleed.

Even the smallest thing can drive a wedge between you and your partner. The first time you find the toothpaste without a top, you replace it, and you may joke about the gassy present left for you at night under the covers. But if you have to replace the top of the toothpaste every morning and take to wearing a gas-mask to bed, you might well start getting a little pissed off. So, sort out small things straight away or they'll keep growing and in time will become a mountain of a problem to deal with.

OK, time out, as they say. Let's check the reality of the problem. What's the gripe about looking after a baby compared to bombs going off and killing people? With people dying every day in poverty, on the scale of things your problem with bottle-feeding looks small. On a personal level and in many homes throughout the country, how do depression, separation, divorce and, in extreme situations, cruelty to children sound?

Understanding what may be dished up on your plate will help you cope. Don't mix rules up with pre-baby ideas about what you thought it was going to be like or the way you thought you'd do things when you started looking after the baby. You will lose the pre-baby ideas faster than someone who's passed their driving test drops their copy of the Highway Code in the bin.

So what are your rules?

Example: I'll hold off giving my child sweets and I'll make my own fresh baby food. Yes, we all start off on that little bandwagon. Well, let me tell you, when Granny gives Baby a piece of chocolate because she likes the way his little lips move when he sucks it, that day your pre-baby ideas and your first rule will be shot to hell. From that day on, no matter how well you purée the banana or carrot, it won't get past Baby's lips, let alone into its stomach.

Home-made baby food doesn't depend on how good the cook is. It depends on how long you can keep Granny from coming round with the chocolate. If you really want to spend your precious free time chopping and puréeing carrots, good luck. But for how long? To jar or not to jar, that is the question: whether it is nobler to cook, chop and purée than suffer the screams and anguish of an outraged baby at feeding time.

At feeding time, most new parents find that their preconceived ideas about feeding disappear out of the window. It is a time when many rules are laid down and then broken, and you may come to realise that it's the baby making headway in what rules will be used today. Any plans or ideas you have now about what you're going to think, do or say when it comes to looking after your baby are as useful as a used nappy.

And while babies may bend the rules, others will destroy them. Perhaps grandparents do these things to get their own back for something their own parents did to them, or because of the sleepless nights they had with you. Or, it could be just something they chuckle about at bedtime. I mean, it will be many years before someone calls me Granddad (if I live that long), but I'm already making plans. I won't babysit so that they can have an evening out or a weekend off, and I'll keep the chocolate and biscuits on a very low coffee table.

So grab some paper and a pen and write down some pre-baby rules. Put it away safely and dig it out in a few years' time. It will probably make you laugh. To help you out, here are a few of mine, which came and went.

Rules of the House
1. The baby will be part of our life, not take away from things we did before.
Some years later: I'm sorry to put it this way, but you have no fucking idea of the time and commitment a baby demands. It's not a part of your life; it takes over all of it. As for the things you did before, now you have no effing time to do them, and it's so long since you did them you can't remember what they were in the first place.

2. We will get a sleeping pattern.
We've all bent over backwards on this one. This rule will be on your list, if not now, then within a year or two. If you'd like a laugh, read up on this sleeping thing. Waste some hours of your free time by finding out what you're doing wrong, then throw the book in the bin and find yourself a comfortable sofa, because you'll be spending many nights sleeping on it.

3. Stimulate the baby every day to help his development.
This is all well and good, but if two people are separated by a generation gap – one is zero and the other thirty – you can begin to see a problem. It's not that your child is getting

brighter, it's that your level of intelligence has dropped after years of reading *Postman Pat* and singing, 'Pat-a-cake, pat-a-cake, baker's man, / Bake me a cake as fast as you can.' Baby likes the song about the fatter cat and the biker man and understands that if he wants to be a postman he needs to get a cat. Stimulation can become repetition, and you find yourself longing for adult conversation. You're even happy to talk to cold callers on the phone conducting market research. You don't give a monkey's for the product and you may make your answers up just to keep them talking and make yourself appear more interesting. But, because they're another adult, you feel that you can talk on the same level, they won't start crying and you don't have to sing to them.

4. No sweets just to keep the children happy.

Many parents use sweets as a means of controlling a child's behaviour: 'If you're good you can have a sweet.' Using sweets in this way just happens – please don't beat yourself over the head about it. Sweets are a way of purchasing peace for five minutes. Keep control of the consumption by all means, but with the odds stacked in the chocolates' favour, your supporters for keeping control will disappear fast.

5. Talk over ideas together.

Setting down this rule means you're still thinking in terms of the relationship you have now, which is without children. If you want to go on holiday, you both look over the holiday brochures, and you have deep discussions together on the best way to do up the house. When the baby plan swings into action, the time you have to talk to your partner about anything other than the baby becomes less and less. After a year or two you just grunt your ideas at each other. Example: 'What do you think about re-doing the bathroom?' 'Uh.' 'How was your day?' 'Uh ug.'

6. No smacking or shouting.

At some point, you'll fall into the trap of using these two parenting skills, which society today dictates as no-nos. I, personally, am on the fence with this one. Over the past eleven years I've smacked Aaron about five times and Kate, who is seven, about three times. My overriding rule about smacking is that I never do it in anger. Like any threat that's repeated and used too often, it can become the norm and the only thing that increases with frequency is intensity, and that's dangerous. I'm not a saint and put my hands up to losing it when the frustration of a bad day has pushed me to my limits. But I always made sure the baby was safe in the cot or playing with some toys while Daddy went down to the kitchen to punch the cupboard door.

7. Freeze breast milk to feed the baby in the daytime.

'Breast is best,' they say, and if you can keep your baby happy with the freezing and thawing routine, stick with it. But bear in mind that if you're going to make and freeze home-made baby food as well, you may need a bigger freezer.

8. Do the housework when the baby's having a nap.

This is a great idea. But if your baby's anything like my first-born – who would wake up at the sound of the toilet chain being pulled upstairs when he was asleep downstairs – think again. Big clean-ups can be done when your partner takes the baby out for a while at the weekends, and so can the ironing and bathroom cleaning, because you can get much more done when you're on your own for a few hours. I can tell that this is making you smile. Maybe you've been trying for years to find a hobby or something you could do at the weekends, and now with a baby your weekend hobby has fallen into your lap.

9. Work part-time or from home.

Child-care bills will dig into any little extra you can bring in, but if you can cover it, go for it. I admire the many single mothers out there who do this grind every day. Depending on your partner's workload and hours, you will have to fit into their working week. If your partner's out of the house at 7.45am and not home until 8.30pm, that's what you have to work within. If you've given up work to stay at home, your real choice won't come until the child starts school, and then all you'll have to cope with is working hours between 9am and 3pm, school holidays and more time off when the child is sick.

10. Go on holidays and trips as a family.

I do hope you put this one on your list as it's a great eye-opener. Before you had children, holidays would have had you asking, 'When can we go? Can we do the helicopter trip as well as the midnight boat trip? We could always stay overnight in a local hotel and travel on the next day. Fantastic.' With a family, however, you ask just one thing: 'Why the hell are we here?' As the person who looks after the children, the only thing you get out of going away on holiday is more work. The kids don't like the food, if they miss their favourite TV programme they're inconsolable, and even showing them the fantastic scenery won't bring them out of it. Good job you brought the sweetie tin.

Again, the choice is yours, but if you're the main carer and you look after cooking and cleaning for your family at home, what makes you think you can switch off and rest on holiday? After a few trips, you'll see the light: it's your partner who's getting away from the office or the factory. Your work comes with you and, because you've been bumped out of your routine, you work twice as hard. As for relaxing, a rabbit with hypertension that is staring into the headlights of an oncoming car is more relaxed. If it's a rest you need, get your partner to take the kids out for the day while you go out and rent a video and grab a bag of chips and a bottle of wine. Back home, you can put your feet up and relax. Don't think about anything. Just put on the video – preferably a film that takes the thinking power of a goldfish – and switch off for ninety minutes.

Chapter 5

Octopus in a Bag

Getting to grips with a routine as soon as possible is important. One routine that is repeated many times in a single day is dressing your baby. Someone once told me that changing a baby is like trying to put an octopus in a string bag.

Stopping the octopus escaping through the holes feels impossible – I think that's a good description. The baby will enjoy the game more when they have the incentive of messing around while you're trying to get control of their frantically moving head, feet, arms and toes.

Men have not been portrayed in a good light when it comes to coping with the practical side of looking after a baby. Many a Hollywood scriptwriter has penned the downfall of a man when he tries to change and dress a baby, and it was funny when they used three men to look after one baby. At the other extreme, men are portrayed as heroes, able to punch and kick their way out of trouble or get up and fight after taking a beating from a room full of bad guys, when such a beating would have most of us unconscious on the pavement with a face like yesterday's pizza. Small wonder, then, that most women think that men need anger-management courses and that they're unable to handle changing a nappy.

I had great fun getting my little octopus dressed. When I use the word 'fun' I promise I'm not pulling your leg. Having a newborn is great because for the most part they'll lie still and let you put on the clean clothes. The hard part is dealing with the fact that they are so small and you feel that if you breathed too heavily you'd break them. You put their tiny fingers and toes into clothes that seem only one size up from an Action Man outfit. The scale is wrong and you feel like King Kong with one hand around their whole body; they are tiny Fay Wrays trying to escape as King Kong carries them up the side of a building.

Buttons and boxing gloves

Within a few months, however, the octopus in your baby grows. As each day passes, their strength and speed develop and as the movements grow, so does the difficulty of dealing with the limbs the baby puts in your way. The baby turns more and more into the octopus and the string bag you're trying to put them in is made of nappies, socks, vests and tops. Every article of clothing takes on a new life of its own and the simple act of putting anything on, over or round the baby has both of you tired and feeling that Rubik's cube was easier to deal with. You do enjoy seeing your baby in what makes them look so cute, which can be anything as long as it has Velcro fastening and an elastic waistband. I personally believe that people who put buttons on baby clothes are sick, twisted people who gain pleasure from the idea. I mean, when you put on a shirt in the morning, you don't do it up while jumping up and down, do you? No, it's with relaxed movements of your hands working in harmony that you do up the buttons. To do the same job on a baby would be like trying to do your shirt up having just been pushed out of an aeroplane. You might get the job done in the end, but with the ground rushing up at you at 150mph, your fingers would feel as supple as bricks and your hands would feel like they were trapped in boxing gloves filled with water.

So, as you put your baby's arm into a clean jacket, his other arm is free to remove other articles of clothing. Again, this is not a big problem with newborn babies, but when their strength increases and they start to sit up and crawl, it will be. You'll need to find a good chiropractic clinic to have your back and shoulders put back in line after months of leaning over and changing a baby on the floor. So, a good tip for this chapter is: get yourself a changing-table. I know, it's another expense, but you will save a bomb on chiropractor bills.

At first, changing and dressing the baby is bloody hard work. He or she weighs only a few pounds, so why does it feel like a wrestling match? Come on, you're probably thinking, just hold them down with one hand. Well, try this. Grab a pound bag of sugar from the kitchen cupboard and hold it out in front of you for fifteen minutes. After five minutes the blood is draining from your hand, after ten minutes your arm feels like it's about to drop off. When the time's up you can drop the bag of sugar, but you can't drop a baby.

Finding your own way of dealing with the practical bits is mainly done through making mistakes, many of the answers to the problems being so simple that you'll smile about them later. However, you'll have to deal with the months or years it takes for you to come up with the solutions.

Rock 'n' roll baby

Here's one example for you. Aaron had the idea that to rock his whole body from side to side was what the changing-mat was made for. He did it whenever I took hold of his legs to lift his bottom off the mat to clean him. The rocking seemed like fun to him, but the smearing it created was amazing. Maybe one day I should have changed him on an artist's canvas, framed it and given it a title like *Emotion* or something. It would not have looked out of place in the Tate Modern. I tried wiping in time with the roll of his body, giving him a toy to hold and calling or making silly noises to him. Now, I know that he enjoyed the freedom of having his nappy off and that most babies enjoy rolling and kicking without a nappy on. But, unless you're working on ideas for the next Turner Prize, a clean bottom is a good idea *before* you let your baby rock and roll over the mat. After months of trying ideas out, I found that the answer was to lay my leg across his body as I did the wiping. With this wrestling hold I got him cleaned in seconds. Like releasing an over-wound rubber band, taking my leg away was the trigger for a frantic kicking, rocking and rolling frenzy. His happiness at having the freedom to do some turbo-kicking was written all over his face and accompanied by noises of enjoyment. (Within a few years, to achieve the same joy would take a few hundred pounds spent on a PlayStation and games.)

Sometimes the problem with the changing may be the place and the length of time you have. When there's plenty of time, things go well. But, as often as not, it's just as you lift the freshly changed baby into the supermarket shopping trolley that you smell the unannounced arrival of yet another badly needed nappy change. You start searching for a clean, dry and private place to do it. This could be in the store if they have a baby-changing room or in the car park, using the back shelf of the car or the open car boot.

The boot idea works, and I've changed my children's nappies many times that way. But be warned that whenever you use the boot, it *will* be raining. You may be enjoying the hottest summer's day in years, but as you lay your baby down, it will start to rain. Using one of the quietest parts of the car park, with no-one near you, you begin, but, just as you open the nappy, someone will pull into the bay next to you. For the rest of the shopping trip, you will see this person in every part of the shop. You may take your time around the vegetable section, but they will catch you up when you get to the fresh meat counter. For the next hour, or however long you are shopping, an invisible embarrassment rope links you to each other.

With all this nappy-changing, the baby's changing-bag becomes a househusband's obsession. You check the contents more frequently than someone checks their suitcase before going on holiday. You pack the bag with all the kit: wipes, nappy sacks, nappies, clean clothes, bottles, dummy, powder or creams, but there'll always be something you left behind. Without the comfort of being at home with everything to hand, you take on the appearance and actions of a drowning man. To others, it's just a bag, but to you it's a lifeline, your life-jacket, which has become part of you, and going out successfully without the support of the changing-bag is as realistic as the withdrawal method is in birth control.

The way forward?

Sometimes the simple act of dressing a child can be overwhelming. From the clean nappy that's refilled before you've put the baby's socks on, to the buttons on that cute little top that will not go through the buttonholes today. They went through with no problems last Saturday when you went to the park. So why not today? Did the buttonholes shrink in the wash? Have the buttons expanded in the heat of the airing cupboard? Or have the sick, twisted sadists at the button factory come up with a shape-changing button? No, it's because the baby's been crying and you've had less sleep than a junior doctor working Saturday night in A&E. You start panicking, because you won't make it to the bank if you don't get out of the house in the next fifteen minutes, your fingers feel like bunches of bananas and it's Wednesday. That's why. It's just because it's fucking Wednesday.

Cleaning and dressing the baby can have the best of us running around like headless chickens from time to time. But as the years go by, your child will take on some of the work and, to some degree, dress themselves. OK, it might be that the top is inside out and the socks don't match, but after years of pulling it off, putting it on and doing it up, you won't care.

Before I end this chapter and find out how many swear words I'll have to cut, I'd like you to think about how many of our problems with looking after a baby have been dealt with better by other creatures on this planet (not including seahorses). Animals may well have a better idea about this child-care thing. They don't have to wear clothes for a start – no fighting with baby-grows or nappies for them. You're born with your birthday suit and you stay in it for the rest of your life. I've never seen a horse trying to explain to its foal that those are the hooves you were born with, that's the only colour they come in and they don't have flashing lights when you trot. If a puppy needs to go, any corner of the garden will do. A nappy? What's that? Just dump anywhere. I'm not a naturist and, with a figure like mine, there must be a law somewhere that would stop me being one, anyway. But apart from the expense of having to move to a warmer climate, it's an idea that has some good points.

Chapter 6

☾ Who Sleeps through the Night and with Whom?

Babies' sleep has been a talking point for parents from as far back as the very first conception at the time of the caveman, right up to modern times with us househusbands. The truth of the matter is your partner sleeps with the baby and you spend the night on the sofa.

New parents spend hundreds of pounds buying something for the baby to sleep in, from a Moses basket to a cot and then a bed. Why? The little darlings are as likely to spend much time in them as a lottery jackpot winner is to work their full two weeks' notice. A good tip is to save the money you'd spend on cots and Moses baskets etc., buy a new mattress for your old double bed, and spend a few hundred pounds on a new sofa and sleeping bag.

People are full of ideas on how you should get your baby to sleep through the night. I'm sure you have heard many stories from friends and family about how little sleep they got the other night because little Johnny kept them awake. If you don't have children, you may say that you're sorry to hear that, with a fake sympathetic look on your face, but you may well be thinking: for God's sake, get a life. It's only a baby. Just keep the baby up for longer and when they're tired they'll sleep.

Many people who haven't got children make that type of comment. And parents often say, 'If you had children you'd understand.' That's true up to a point, but my reply would be, 'If you had a child who didn't sleep and cried most of the time, you'd understand a lot better.'

One of the hardest things to come to terms with is the fact that some babies sleep well and some don't. If your baby won't sleep, you can grab and read all the information about the subject you can get your depressed little hands on, and you may come to the conclusion that you're doing something wrong. You're not. You just have a baby that likes to cry and not sleep. As long as the baby is clean, dry, fed and not ill, that's it, that's the black-and-white of the baby-sleeping story. You're in one camp or the other. This may go on for a few months or a few years – it's the luck of the draw, and it's the hand you've been dealt. Or if you like, it's your own gold-plated fan with a few years' supply of shit that you can throw at it. Note: people use the term 'baby's sleep pattern' as though babies follow some type of rule. This is bollocks. Do you know why? Because they don't have one. A baby can fall asleep with a wet, shit-filled nappy, strapped in a high chair if they want to. But you could put them down in a nice comfortable cot with a soothing tape of whale song playing and with a fluffy bunny mobile turning above their head, and they still wouldn't go to sleep.

After an hour, your back's breaking because you've been leaning over the cot too long giving encouraging sleep talk. 'Ah, baby go sleepy, sleep now, ah, look at the bunnies they're sleeping, good night, my darling, good night, good night.' As you step out of the warm, cosy bedroom, the floorboard you've been meaning to fix groans like a door in an old horror film. From the cot comes a loud shrill that fills the air. Your heart sinks and your back clicks in anticipation of yet another hour of cot torment. Yes, you need your sleep. But at this moment, with that pain in your back getting stronger and the acid building in your stomach, you also need a couple of painkillers and a handful of indigestion tablets.

It is true that newborn babies sleep a lot. Do you believe me? Would you buy double-glazing from me? No, well, I can see that. 'Newborn' means the few days between birth and when you get them home from the hospital. Most sleep a lot in this time, but not at the times your body clock has been working on for years. And as far as newborn babies' sleeping goes, a few short weeks or months – if you're lucky – of good sleep count for nothing, if the next five years are hell. Now, about them windows…

Don't wake the baby!

With your first baby, you'll do anything you can just to get them to sleep. At first, you let the baby fall asleep on your lap as you cuddle them. 'Oh dear, Baby likes this.' That's a trap we've all fallen into. If the baby gets used to falling asleep on your lap, that's the pattern they'll want to stick with for the next few years. Around this time, you'll notice big changes taking place in your body. New parents take the next evolutionary step. Apart from your worsening indigestion and the larger and larger bags under your eyes, your hearing is now as acute as a bat's. You can hear your baby starting to wake up in the next room, and you notice just how noisy your neighbours and the area where you live have become. To add to your problems, you feel you have the only baby who cries all the time. You hear stories about people whose babies sleep right through the night and don't cry until they need their morning feed. So, again, you beat yourself over the head because you feel you must be doing something wrong. No, you aren't. As I said, it's just the hand you've been dealt.

Your anxiety about the situation will keep you awake while your baby sleeps, as will the fear that anything may wake them; you sometimes go to extreme lengths to stop that happening by taking an interest in the noise of those everyday things and objects around you. (I've stuffed the doorbell chimes with tissue paper to stop them ringing too loudly and waking the baby.) People often say that a baby picks up on the frame of mind of the person holding them. Well, so do *things* when a baby gets near them. Objects work against you – even your house can take on a life of its own. Before we had a baby, the closing of doors never went through our minds. If I needed the toilet I just opened the door, walked in, closed the door and used the toilet. Coming out was just as simple: trousers up, flush the toilet, wash my hands, open the door, walk out. It was so easy then. Now everything seemed to be working against me, and everything and everyone seemed hell-bent on waking the baby.

You take the phone off the hook so its ringing won't wake the baby. When you do sit down, you relax by watching the TV with subtitles on and the volume off, just in case the soundtrack wakes the baby. Now, with the baby asleep, you start to hear voices, and you think: I'm cracking up. Still, the good side to this is that if you're hearing voices, and if you're lucky, one of them might be God. This could be your chance to ask the question we all want to know the answer to: God, why are we here? Feeling that it's quite possible you've gone mad, you ask the question anyway. The voice answers you, telling you to 'Please hang up and try again.' Back in the real world with a bang, you rush over to the phone and put the receiver back in its cradle. You pray, 'Oh, please don't wake up yet.' This is a Catch-22 situation. If you go upstairs to see whether all is well, the top two steps and the landing floorboards will creak, and the noise will wake the baby.

I've lost count of the times I had to go upstairs to the toilet and, just as my foot left the floor, the floorboard creaked – and the next second the baby was crying. My toilet freedom only came from the rose bush in the garden. Imagine pissing in the garden because of the fear that walking upstairs and making the door and floorboards creak may wake the baby! When it comes to a choice between rose bush and more hours of crying, the rose bush gets the short straw.

Babies wake up because of noise or movement but, just to make your life interesting, it isn't every noise or movement – some noises and some movements actually send the baby to sleep. This leaves you on a knife-edge, wondering which is which. After six months with no sleep, the bags under your eyes are so large that they're dragging on the carpet. You know everything that will wake your baby, but you still can't make sense of it, or understand why what sent them to sleep in the past now has them crying.

You would think scientists would have dealt with this sleep thing by now. I mean, you turn on the radio or television and someone somewhere is telling you that research teams, based in a part of the country you have never heard of before and with an annual budget in the millions, have discovered something. You know the sort of thing: you can get a nice boiled egg in three minutes, but boil it for five minutes and the yolk goes hard; there will be more cars on the road in ten years' time; and the Big Bang may have happened a million years earlier than they thought. Who gives a rat's arse? Give us something useful like a translator that can help the baby understand that it's 3am and Mummy and Daddy need to go bye-byes.

OK, here's the key and the answer you need: babies sleep when they want to. All you have to do is put your life on hold and accept that you're going to feel like hell for the next few years.

'Oh no, Mr Charlton, you shouldn't say that. With the right information and understanding, any baby can learn to get a good sleep pattern. May I suggest to your readers a warm evening bath with their baby to relax them, and maybe some lavender oil and calming crystals in the bedroom?'

'No! Fuck off!'

Let's get back on this planet.

When Aaron was a baby, he fell asleep while eating dinner in his high chair and I had to wake him to get the last bit of food out of his mouth so he didn't choke. I suppose it was a bit like falling asleep after Sunday dinner, when the sofa is the only thing you can cope with. So the comfort of being warm and fed will help bring on sleep. Moving a baby won't be a problem when they're out like a light, but until they are, they can be woken by anything. To a baby, a closing door has the same shock value as a cell door closing for the first time on a prisoner sent down for ten years.

An exhaust-ing night

I think it's fair to say at this point that, along with the lack of sleep, you'll notice a big drop in your tolerance of other people. Things you took in your stride in the past become intolerable. One of the many examples that spring to mind is one night with a revving car. A few houses away from us, a guy was doing up an old American car. I don't know the make, but it was big, blue and did about two miles to the gallon. Late one night with some friends, he decided that it would be a good idea to run this thing up in his garage. I don't think the exhaust was connected, because the volume the car revved at was like an aeroplane taking off. Our front windows rattled with each rev of the engine. I went into the back garden and called out, 'Do you know what time it is?' More revving was the only reply. I started shouting my request and other neighbours came out into their gardens and voiced their disapproval as well. The revving stopped; the neighbours and I went back inside.

I sat down in the front room, not feeling comfortable at all. I was angry, pissed off at people's lack of consideration for others. I hadn't even had time to get my shoes off when the revving started again. The noise was unbelievable. I went ballistic. In seconds I was standing beside this revving monster. The bonnet was up and the car's owner had his head under it, drooling over the power of the engine. The noise was so loud that it was a few seconds before he and his friends knew I was there. 'Turn that fucking thing off!' I exploded. With the aid of a shovel leaning against the garage wall, I demonstrated that if I heard that car one more time that night, I'd come back with an axe and smash every window of the car and personally chop the effing revving engine out of his effing car.

Like many guys, I have had occasion to fight back in the past. This was one of the few times when I really did not give a toss about the consequences. After the stress of putting up with a crying baby for days on end, dealing with five guys and remodelling the revving monster would have been a picnic for the shovel and me. Fortunately within a few days apologies from both sides prevented any long-term problems arising from the incident.

I'm not anti-car: in fact, when it comes to getting a baby to sleep, being in a car can work wonders. The movement of the car and the rumble of the wheels can rock a baby to sleep. I spent many a late night doing the car sleep run, waving to fellow househusbands as we roamed the A10 and the A406 waiting for the bundle of joy to drop off on the back seat.

There aren't many things you can be sure of in this life – that is, apart from death and the fact that the Jehovah's Witnesses always knock on your door when it's your turn for a Sunday morning lie-in. Many will criticise how you deal with your baby when it comes to bedtime, but the only people who matter are you, the baby and your partner. If walking the streets at night with the baby in a pushchair will get them to sleep, fine. If driving them around in the car breaks the crying pattern, do it. I could fill pages and pages with the rubbish the experts tell you about how you should get your baby to sleep through the night. But there are as many expert ideas as there are rat droppings in the London sewers. With a baby you may have no choice but to work through it together and in whatever way works for you. After all, a few hours' sleep, even if it is on the sofa, is much better than no sleep at all.

Chapter 7

 Teething and Chewing the Woodwork

If you've stuck with the job of househusband for long enough to be looking after your baby full-time when they start teething, well done. And as for the smug ones out there whose babies have slept well and have been little angels at night, things are gonna change. If, on the other hand, you're going through the teething thing with your baby at the moment, you may find it helpful to look forward to when your baby grows up and leaves home.

Most babies suffer when teething and in most of them the signs of teething are clear: from red cheeks that glow in the dark to dribbling that can be measured in pints. The baby's clothes are soaking wet from neck to nappy line. But before the signs become clear, you can be sent into a bit of a panic because the baby is crying more than normal. 'What's normal?' you ask. If your baby cries a lot anyway, you may miss the early signs and go straight into the glowing cheeks and Olympic dribbling event. If your baby, so far, has been a pleasant little bundle of joy, the fourteen-pound sledgehammer of reality is going to hit you right in the face.

It's funny how life turns you round. When you're seventeen, all you want is to get a car of your own and lose your virginity. In your twenties, ending up in a job you enjoy would be fantastic, getting some money together to put down a deposit on a flat, holidays with your friends, drinking, eating out, talking over the world's problems and putting them right, and of course more bonking. A few years later, you're holding a screaming baby and you're desperate. You're panicking. Where is it? You'd cut off your right arm, sell your soul to find it. All the dreams and the world's problems you were going to put right just a few years earlier have turned to bollocks. The baby's screaming has reached a peak. '*Where is it?*' you scream at the empty house. You remember it's in the other bag in the bathroom. You put the baby down on the sofa and run upstairs. Bang! Your big toe hits the first step; it's not until you get into the bathroom that the pain of the split toenail hits you. 'For fuck's sake!' (a much-used phrase for househusbands, which helps release built-up stress and is itself a form of pain relief). You grab the bag and hop downstairs on your good leg. You're in full baby-panic mode; you pull the sides of the bag so hard that the zip bursts open, spilling clean nappies, creams and wipes. 'Where is it?' You feel desperately through the bag – cotton buds, clean bottles, nappy sacks, an empty calorie-counter sandwich box – your fingertips make contact with the familiar metal tube – you've got it! Hallelujah, your luck's in! The blue tube is in your hand and being opened. You no longer hear the baby crying as you bathe in the joy and relief of the moment. You squeeze some of the teething gel onto your finger, then gently rub it into the gums of the screaming, red-faced, drooling lunatic on the sofa.

Brilliant Bonjela!

In the past, you may have thought that the first man landing on the moon was inspiring and pushed science to its limits or, perhaps, you still remember your greatest feelings, like your first kiss. Well, for someone with a teething baby, Bonjela teething gel is one of the greatest things ever invented. The relief when the baby is no longer screaming its head off because of pain is wonderful and comes a pretty close second to my first French kiss under a road bridge in Richmond, I can tell you. I don't want this to read like a product placement, but I would like to try and put the point over to people who can't grasp how important teething gel is. Bonjela is a life-saving gel that has househusbands saying, 'If I ever meet the person who invented Bonjela I'll kiss them – male or female.' To give you the right perspective, if I met an astronaut, I'd shake his hand. See the difference?

With the baby now much calmer on the sofa, the panic of the past ten minutes ebbs away. Yes, just ten minutes, that's how long the whole thing lasted, and you've been running around like a headless chicken again. Still holding the Bonjela, you sit down and relax against the sofa. The baby is being kind to you, lying still and sucking hard on their teething ring (another good piece of equipment for the teething survival kit). Mind you, after a screaming fit like that, your poor little bundle of joy will need the rest to get its strength back.

With the house now at peace, your brain can relay other forgotten bits of information faster than a racing-car heading for the finish line. The nerve-endings in your big toe are sending pain messages back to your brain and your eyes confirm the information: there's blood oozing through your sock. As you remove your sock, you also remove the left half of your big toenail. It hurts, but if the baby were screaming you wouldn't be feeling a thing. From this day on, you have Bonjela tubes all over the house, from the first-aid box to kitchen cupboards and on bookshelves – you always have one within arm's reach. If you go out, you have one in your left pocket and one in your right pocket, one in the car, one in the pushchair and, just in case, one more in the changing-bag.

As I mentioned, a teething ring is a handy piece of equipment the baby can bite down on (sorry, that should be 'can gum down on'). The ring helps with cutting their teeth. The one that Aaron liked was one you could put in the fridge to chill, and the coldness helped numb the pain. He also enjoyed attacking the woodwork in the house. His best trick was to pull himself up on the door of the dining-room cupboard that housed my stereo and CDs. As the door opened, his little hands would grab the top of the door and his mouth began working on the beaded edge of the door. I'm sure I've got a photo somewhere of him doing this. His fingertips just made it over the edge of the door (a bit like those trick fingers you sometimes see stuck onto a car boot, as if someone's trapped inside) and only the top of his head moved as his gums were in full contact with the woodwork. The wetness from his dribbling would expand the top of the wooden door so it wouldn't close until the next morning, when it had dried out. Some years later, when Aaron could understand things like 'It's not nice to chew through Daddy's CD cupboard', I showed him the marks he'd made when he was teething. Teething is a difficult time but, unless your partner's given birth to some type of sucking fish that has no teeth, it's a time you will just have to get through.

Chapter 8

❗ Spiritual Enlightenment

We are all struck with times in our lives that make us question the meaning of the one we've been born into. If you're religious, this may help you to understand your part and the role you'll play while on this planet.

This chapter is not about househusbands finding God, because an agnostic like myself does not have that comfort, though I do call out to God and his son many times in a crisis, hoping for enlightenment. (To date, he's never spoken to me; maybe he's out burying dinosaur bones to keep testing the faith of those fundamentalist Christians out there.)

The chapter is more about what level of stress will drive you to wish to play no more part in the future of this planet. I once told a friend (who'd just become a father for the first time) that his life would feel like a rocket on Bonfire Night.

'What do you mean?' he asked.

I told him, 'The lit blue touch paper represents your birth, the orange glow after lighting the rocket represents your life from one to ten years, and the pre-launch fizzing accounts for years ten to twenty. The rest of your life will be the flash of the speeding rocket as it zooms skywards.'

If your life has been fulfilling and you have touched the lives of a lot of people, the climax to the rocket's flight would be an explosion of colour. Someone like William Shakespeare or Gandhi would light up the sky for miles, the cascade of colours and glittering stars from their rocket so bright that it would illuminate the world and be seen by millions of people. The househusband's rocket on the other hand is the small cheap one you sometimes get in those boxes of mixed fireworks. You know, the ones where the whole lot have less explosive firepower than a box of matches. When the househusband's rocket is lit, it soars to the height of the second-floor bedroom window and then just goes out – no cascades of colour with this one. You may, however, see a glow from the burnt rocket stick as it falls back and lands at your feet.

'Oh dear, Alan is feeling a little bit down.'

Never mind, and to anyone out there who's interested, remember he's available for after-dinner speeches and for children's parties.

I'm making the point that at some times in your life you question things, and if you're doing full-time child-care, that questioning comes round sooner than for most people. At some point you will sit down and think, what the hell am I doing here? This is driving me crazy. I'm not the same person I was, and I'm getting pissed off over the smallest of things. In the same way that someone with a bad back always finds themselves dropping things and a person with a bad foot will always have that one stood on as they wait in the queue at the bank, with a baby, you can feel like you have a slipped disc, an ingrown toenail plus a migraine, all with the overwhelming feeling that it's you who are doing something wrong. Happy families are all over the place, aren't they? Well, what's going wrong with mine, and why am I the only person feeling this way? I need a way out, or at least a larger and longer-lasting rocket, 'for fuck's sake' (I told you this was a tried and tested househusband phrase).

As with most things that drive you crazy, the feeling of being out of control of events and of the situation building up around you only adds to the problem. It can be anything from queuing in the supermarket or driving in heavy traffic to the baby not giving you five minutes' peace so you can use the toilet. All of which may add so much stress that sometimes you wonder where it all could possibly have come from. The stressometer shows that your stress levels got higher when the baby was born and higher still once you started looking after him.

I know you're thinking that a baby brings warmth and love into a relationship and, yes, looking back over the years from the point I'm at in my life now, I have to agree. But for many of us the good bits feel very small at the time, and when you're out of your depth looking after a baby, they can even seem tiny. They could live in a tiny house in a tiny street, in a tiny country, on a tiny planet, in a tiny corner of a bloody big, fucking stressful universe. Keeping this happy thought in mind reminds me of one day of stress, which went just a little crazy.

Out of my way, stressed dad coming through!
When Aaron was a baby, most weeks I tried to get over to see my mum and dad for a few hours. The journey was a pig – I had to drive right across London – but I avoided the rush hour and that made the drive about an hour each way. Apart from land mines going off, because my parents were obsessed with giving Aaron a chocolate biscuit as soon as we got through the door, it was a helpful and welcome change of scene. We had a great time, with Mum and Dad playing with Aaron in the garden, and Mum showing her grandson off to the neighbours.

On this particular day, I stayed a bit longer than usual and had to drive back in the rush hour. Aaron was soon fast asleep in his car seat in the back of the car – I always tried to time the drive back from my parents' home for when he was due a sleep. Because London traffic is so bad, it was easier for him to sleep on the journey, which left me free to fight with all the other London drivers trying to make headway.

After thirty minutes, I knew this was going to be a bad traffic day. We've all felt frustration build up in a traffic jam. If you're late for an appointment, or maybe an interview for a new job, that adds to the stress, with the cars in front stuck fast and, by the looks of it, not going to be moving for some time. Your stressometer moves to a higher level and is the only thing that's moving in this traffic.

An hour and a half after leaving my parents' house, we were still ten miles from home. Aaron had slept most of that time, and for the past thirty minutes had been an angel, amusing himself by sucking his dummy and chewing the corner of his jacket. He was teething, and there was so much dribble running down his jacket that its colour was now two shades darker.

I was stuck in the middle of three lanes of traffic. Two hours of moving slower than a snail would move in a salt mine. And then Aaron's crying started. His nappy needed changing and he'd been stuck in a car seat for two hours. We could go nowhere; I kept turning round to talk to him and passing him things to play with. There was no turn-off in sight. If I could only just pull over and find some shops or a petrol station, I could clean Aaron up and have a break for a few minutes; that would ease the situation.

The traffic was painfully slow. I was doing everything I could to keep Aaron happy, and just hoping we could turn off the A406 soon. Another fifteen minutes and we must have moved less than half a mile, but I could see a petrol station up ahead. To drivers with small children in the car, a petrol station is an oasis. All I had to do now was get out of the middle lane and across the inside lane onto the turn-off.

With the other car drivers fighting for every inch of tarmac, moving forward and across to the turn-off was done inch by inch. My car indicators were flashing like mad, but they were invisible to everyone else, because other drivers only look ahead in traffic, fearing that if they make eye contact, they may have to give way. No one was looking at me and no one was giving way.

My frustration and anger were past their sell-by date, I'd hit the limit on the stressometer and I lost it; I was trapped inside a metal box with four rubber tyres and a windscreen.

Relief came from head-butting the doorframe of the car. I could feel my forehead starting to swell, but carried on with the stress relief. *Bang! Bang!* More relief. The noise of bone meeting metal must have been even louder outside the car than inside, because it attracted the attention of my fellow motorists. As I said before, I'm not a spiritual man, but what happened next was like a biblical moment – the parting of the Red Sea was nothing compared to the traffic moving out of the way for the lunatic in the blue Ford, with indicators flashing a warning that he was coming through, and anyone who didn't want to eat their food through a straw for the next few months should get out of his way.

More relief came as I pulled into the petrol station forecourt. The sight of a man with a swollen, blood-stained forehead asking if he could use the washroom to change the baby's nappy may have seemed a little out of the ordinary. But a London petrol station attendant will have worked the Friday and Saturday night shift at some time, and will have dealt with all the Neanderthals coming out of the clubs and pubs. Compared to people like that, I must have looked quite normal. The attendant gave me the key for the washroom and I set to work changing Aaron's nappy and cleaning him up. On leaving the washroom I grabbed a cold drink and something for Aaron and thanked the attendant. I took Aaron out to the car and just walked around with him for about fifteen minutes. He was smiling, as if being outside the car seemed good to him as well.

It was a nightmare of a journey and I'm sure many of you have experienced road rage in some form. How you deal with it is personal to you, but let it go if you can or it may build up until you explode over the smallest thing, just because it was the last straw. For me, physical release was the pressure-relief valve. Aggression, frustration, fear or anger might build up over a long time but could be released in a second. That release was always done to myself or a nearby door, kitchen cupboard or the doorframe of my car. This stress-relief technique could come back and haunt me, especially when I tried to sell things:

'Hi. I've come about the car you're selling, the blue one on the forecourt.'

'Oh yes, sir,' replies the salesman, 'this is a good car. It's a good runner with a service history, and the bodywork's in good condition... well, apart from the dented, blood-stained interior on the driver's side.'

'Oh, my God! Was the driver hurt in a crash?'

'No, sir, the last owner was a househusband.'

Physical stress relief helped me a lot. In our house there was a cupboard under the stairs with a strong wooden door. Whenever I found myself getting near exploding point, I'd deliver a hard right cross to my friendly stress-relieving toy. In fact, I think there might be a market for a pad you could fit to a wall in your home, office or car and whenever you needed to explode, you could just hit the pad.

You may condemn me for the way I reacted in the traffic jam, but I don't give a toss. I wasn't merely late for dinner or a job interview. I had a screaming, teething baby on the back seat, something which at times made me a nervous wreck, a person who I didn't like any more. A person who sometimes felt lost and alone, just when all around him friends, family and society were telling him how wonderful the whole thing was. You could say that hitting walls and doors was a primitive release of frustration and emotion, basic and deep-rooted. But it's still something we have to control, cover up and lie about, because it's seen as wrong and a weakness. I say, as long as it's not people you're hitting, and as long as it helps, enlightenment and release are just a cupboard door away...

Chapter 9

💧 Crying: The Pain of it All

Well, it's great that you've made it this far. This may be for two reasons. You may have found the book enlightening, honest and funny, or perhaps you've just picked it up and are flicking through it. If it's the latter, please buy a copy as I feel old age coming at me fast and need the royalties. If you could find a few hundred thousand more people to buy it, too, that would be fantastic.

I've just had a thought. You might be a producer looking for material for a TV show or for a film. Oh my God, you could be Steven Spielberg! Well, let me say from the off, Mr Spielberg, that I've enjoyed your work for many years and please, please feel free to contact me. I may be a sad househusband at the moment, but I'm hoping to find paid employment soon.

You see, you don't give up hope, even as a househusband. We may well get life, and the enjoyment of it, kicked out of us for a few years, but we're good at hoping for better times. Don't worry, I'm not going to start adding shark attacks, UFOs, dinosaurs, or cars being pursued by trucks, just to keep Mr Spielberg happy. No, it's you I'm talking to, telling you the way it is and letting you know that you can get through it.

So let's get back to the real stuff. I'd like to talk over some points about the role your baby's crying can play in your relationships with your baby and with your partner. For some people, a crying baby doesn't seem to be a problem – they can carry on and take the baby's crying in their stride, while others find that the crying almost destroys them. For me, a baby's crying is a sound that has evolved over thousands of years to be as upsetting as possible. Yes, I've been told it's the only way a baby can communicate, but that doesn't take away the fact that, to me, a crying baby can bring on the same trauma as having my testicles scraped along the coarse-cutting side of a blunt cheese grater.

You may think that I'm a bit harsh comparing the pain of a crying baby to a DIY vasectomy with a kitchen utensil. Not so. That's the level of fear and dread I felt when I was on my own with a crying baby. The fact that I was the only adult around and that it was my job to look after the baby only added to my anxiety. When you first start looking after a baby, you think that crying equals pain: if the baby's crying, it must be in pain. The level of pain a baby can inflict just by the volume of its crying is on a level with the pain experienced by a man having his leg sawn off – or a househusband whose wife has just told him she's pregnant again! Unable to deal with any more unexpected blows like that one, he has a choice to make. A little time later, an ambulance is called and he is taken to hospital with severe genital bleeding. He's still holding the cheese grater on his arrival at A&E.

The different levels and tones of a baby's crying can be linked to different problems. You have, the 'I'm hungry' cry, the 'I need changing' cry, the 'I've dropped my toy' cry, the 'Where did Mummy go?' cry, the 'My milk's too cold' cry, the 'My milk's too hot' cry and the 'I'm over-tired' cry. And of course there's the 'Nothing wrong with me, I just feel like being a right bastard today' two-hour non-stop screaming performance. You do get to know the different cries over time, especially the ones that involve eating or changing. On the whole, these two calm down once the mouth is sucking a bottle or the other end is dry and in a clean nappy. Remember to wind the baby after feeding, because if they got so hungry they had to cry for it, the chances are that along with mouthfuls of milk, they'll also have taken in a lot of air.

Party casualty

That reminds me of the time I took Aaron to a party. Not a get-pissed-quick adults' party of the type that ends with people trying to find a late-night kebab or KFC takeaway on the way home, not that type of thing at all. I mean a children's party with balloons, cakes, peanut butter sandwiches and a clown doing tricks for the kids. The party was in full swing; the kids were having a great time, with party games and dancing. (Well, I say 'dancing'. The girls were jigging in time with the music, the boys were doing some form of running that ended up with them diving on the floor.)

I was with a few other parents, standing outside the venue getting away from the noise, talking over the joys of parenthood. Whenever we heard one of the children crying inside the hall, we used our cry-recognition skills to tell whether it was our child and whether the cry was serious or just the kid protesting to the clown that he wanted a balloon sword, not a balloon in the shape of a dog.

The party had been going on for some time when a car pulled up with some latecomers. We all noticed the car because as soon as the doors opened, we could feel the stress that had built up inside during the journey that was now free to escape. Three children of party age jumped out of the car, holding presents. We opened the door of the hall for them and they ran inside, screaming 'Happy birthday' and heading for the cake table. The driver was carrying a baby. His face told the story; images of my nightmare on the A406 flashed through my head. He told us he'd been stuck in traffic for the past hour with his four kids. Four kids? Christ, he had our respect and our sympathy. He said the three older ones had spent the whole journey going on and on about being late for the party, and then, when the traffic did start moving, he had to stop the car to feed the baby, who'd started screaming. I'm sure that if any of us standing there that day had known that poor driver a bit better, we'd have had a group sympathy hug. Just think about it. That guy had suffered three children giving him the works, the 'we're going to be late for the party' cry, and then the baby started up.

Over a cup of coffee that someone brought out to him, we told him that we'd all been through it and he started to relax. We all started talking about being modern-day fathers and the things we had in common, such as sleeping on the sofa, trying to remember the last time you went out for a drink and a curry, or the one night you didn't have to beg for sex from your partner.

But this guy's problems weren't over yet. He was just about at the point of enjoying himself when we heard the pre-vomit sound coming from his baby. That's the noise that results from a speedily drunk bottle of milk, when there's no time available to wind the baby because you're stuck in traffic, you're running late and you're being screamed at from the back seat by three upset party animals.

He only just had time to pass someone his coffee cup and mutter the stress-relieving mantra, 'Oh, for fuck's sake!' before he was covered with what looked like a good six fluid ounces of regurgitated milk. The baby was sick all over his jacket, shirt, face and hair, an inevitable reaction to panic in-car bottle-feeding. The smell was awful. Someone took the baby from him, thinking that maybe this would be the last straw, and that this father might be thinking about drop-kicking the baby across the car park. Someone else fetched water and paper towels and the rest of us grabbed his jacket and shirt from him as he went inside to clean himself up in the toilet. He was not a happy puppy. When he came back out, I remember looking at his face and thinking, he won't forget this day in a hurry.

The crying game: for kids and parents

Crying may not give you the entire story of what's troubling your baby, and this lack of communication skills can send you round in circles. Your baby starts crying, you pick them up, ah, nappy needs changing, abracadabra, it's done. But the baby's still crying. Then it must be time for a feed. No, still crying. Better wind the baby. Still crying, and the pitch and volume are rising. Teething gel and teething ring are applied, but both are spat out. Still crying. Build-up of panic: what's the matter? The baby is now screaming. You make up another feed; the baby isn't interested. Have you done something wrong? You check back over what you've done, and the first thing was a nappy change. When you strip the nappy off, you see that you've caught a bit of the baby's skin in the nappy ties, so, pulling back the old ties, you refit the nappy. Baby stops crying.

Now, I don't know what *you* mean by communication, but in terms of explaining what the problem is, crying's a pretty lousy form of communication as far as helping parents goes. Your tension and frustration at not being able to find out what's upsetting your baby can backfire onto your partner, too. If the usual things – feeding, walking round the room gently, rocking the baby in your arms – don't work, the next step will be a trip in the car to see if that will do the trick. Back at home, your partner walks into the bedroom and asks why the baby's still crying. Your anxiety about the baby's non-stop crying for the past half-hour boils over: 'I Don't Fucking Know Why He's Still Fucking Crying. You Take Him. You Deal With It.' Stunned by this two-barrel verbal attack, your partner makes a run for it, and you sit down on the edge of the bed and cuddle the baby. Within moments, the baby's fast asleep in your arms and all is quiet once more, apart from the sound of your partner crying downstairs.

Your relationship has changed. Each of you feels that you aren't the same person. Many people have commented on why relationships fall apart and, because I don't know you, I would not dream of making a comment about you. You may think I get on my soapbox sometimes, and you may disagree with the ideas I come out with, but they're feelings and ideas that I, and many people I've talked to, have and think about. Now that my children are older, I can enjoy things more, but it's taken years to put back together the pieces of what was a good, happy and loving relationship with Caroline.

Dealing with a crying baby is very hard at times and can make the best of us fall apart. Much of the pain comes from having to guess what your baby wants and what you and your partner need from each other. I wish you the best of luck with all of this, which you will have to go through with your baby. I can only hope that it's an easier roller-coaster ride than mine was.

Chapter 10

Ⓝ Ignoring Chapter 4

It's time to remind ourselves about those rules we were going to make for how we wanted to bring up the baby – I only gave you ten to start with, remember. I'm sitting at the computer thinking about how many you may have written down, and I'm pretty sure you've got up to twenty or thirty.

Just for fun, let's say you put fifty rules on your list. I may or may not be right about that number, but I'll make a pretty good guess at how many are left. I reckon thirty of the fifty rules have gone – in fact, I reckon they went after the first six months. Ten more you're still working on, as they haven't been introduced yet, maybe because the baby hasn't started teething or because you're still talking to the grandparents. Five of the rules you're bending so much that you feel it was pointless writing them down in the first place. The last five are split between you and your partner, and the only part of those five you could call 'working' is the half of one you share. Is that clear? No? Confused? Yes! Well, that's what having children does to you.

After travelling the baby path for some time, you can appreciate the naïve way you started the journey and the way some people always seem to have the idea that they could do it better. You know the sort of people I mean: the ones that often make judgements from their chair. If only they'd get their fat backsides out of their chairs and try it for themselves, they'd have to deal with the consequences. It's easy to criticise when you haven't been through the pain of doing something. Take the comments from fans at a boxing match, for example. Two men in the ring, both of whom train harder in one day than most of the people watching do in a year. Both are at the peak of physical fitness and able to beat the hell out of each other. From ringside, a fan screams that he thinks the champ is a wanker. See what I mean? I'd love to see that fat, flabby, white-fleshed heckler get into the ring. Before he even got his breath back from climbing over the ropes, the sight of the champ coming over would hit him with the reality of the situation and make him fall to his knees, hoping the referee would count very quickly.

Having to look after a baby for a few years is your boxing ring and can make you feel that you're fighting the champ while others tell you what you should be doing and the best way to do it. But they have no idea. They're sitting outside the ring; they aren't feeling the punches and the pain. Now, with a little time under your belt, you know the rules that matter in your household, and as to what some people on the outside tell you, well, you can see those comments for what they really are – bollocks. This chapter is about revisiting your pre-baby ideas, maybe regretting some of them and hopefully enjoying the ones that worked.

I was naïve about the baby and shocked by my feelings of not being able to cope. Does this make me a weak person? Maybe so, but I've learnt a lot about dealing with my problems, about which ones are best dealt with by putting my head in the sand to keep the peace and which ones are the ones to fight back on. Many things I am not strong about dealing with, but getting through it all must count for something.

Many of the rules about bringing up the children and about who does what will depend on your relationship with your partner. Whether it's controlling your child's intake of sweets or the discipline you use in the home, both of you have to agree on a level. The hard part for househusbands is that their role is sometimes different from a mother's role at home. Most men have no idea how hard being at home can be – if they had, a lot of families would work better. For both sexes, the one who goes out to work will, in time, feel that the one at home has the easier option. Having respect for each other's role would be a great rule to write down and carve on tablets of stone. Who knows? You may have made it one of the rules of *your* house, and if you did, I bet it lasted as long as a Mars bar in the hands of a chocoholic. The rules I laid down must have been written on blotting paper, which is OK if it never rains in your world. I know the UK has a lot of rain, but I'm sure north London got more than its fair share in the years 1991 to 1998.

New Rules of the House
1. I will just put up with it.
The golden rule of knowing your place, this one. It helps with many of the others and can develop into 'putting up with it and trying to ignore it'. Yes, it's putting your head in the sand, but other animals are dominated by this rule of family life too – ostriches have been doing it for years.

2. If it goes wrong, I'll relax and start again.
The first part happens a lot: getting things wrong can happen as easily as a househusband can get indigestion. The hard part is staying relaxed and calmly starting again. You can take a bit from the first rule and stick your head in the sand and count to ten or, if it's gone really wrong, count to 389. Oh dear, still not calm? OK, shout at the wall, go for a walk, kick the cat, do some meditation, get away for a few days, take a swimming holiday in Australia or go on a cruise round the world. Take your pick.

3. I will give up even trying to watch the television.

When you can watch the TV will change, depending on whether your baby is asleep or awake. I could have said: 'If you want to watch a TV programme, you'll miss it, and if you tape it you'll lose the tape.' I didn't say that, as I didn't want to upset you too much. The times when you can watch the TV aren't always the times when you want to, so here's a top tip about videos: always have a good supply of films and comedy tapes in the house, because at three o'clock in the morning, with a sleeping baby on your lap, at least there's something you like on the telly.

As parents, of course we have to keep control over what our children watch, not least because as a parent you'll notice just how much the children are hit with advertising.

One thing that gets on my tits is that children's TV presenters always shout. They shout the name of the programme, they shout who won the quiz and they shout the web site and phone number. Is it because shouting is supposed to get across a feeling of excitement, to make up for the poor quality of the programme? Does this tell our children that you can enjoy looking at dog shit as long as you shout about it?

If you think about it for a minute, you'll notice that your viewing time goes down and your disappointment in what you allow your children to see goes up. But the TV licence fee stays the same and you're paying for it. Life's little enjoyments do seem to be getting fewer and fewer, don't they?

4. I will only do DIY when the children are out for the day.

This is a great rule if you enjoy DIY. It's a welcome break from the normal routine of nappies, bottles and sick. Having the family go to see Grandma, so that you can paint and put up shelves for the day – it's like a holiday. For that short time, you're your old self again, doing work that you can see finished at the end of the day and which adds something to the home. But if you don't enjoy DIY, you may find yourself asking 'Why do househusbands have to do all the DIY around the house?'. If the ladies want to go out to work while their men do the looking-after-the-baby thing, they'll need to find out, if they don't already know, about things like the fuse box and how to re-tile the kitchen floor. A stopcock is a valve to turn off the water, not just something that happens in a passionate bedroom when the baby starts crying. So, ladies, if you want your man to look after the kids, cook, clean and do the shopping, and still give you first-class rumpy-pumpy in the bedroom, you'd better start brushing up on your DIY skills. Your first job could be to fix the lock on the bedroom door to stop late-night passion being interrupted by the kids. Who knows? One night you may go into the bedroom and find the bed covered with rose petals with your man lying there looking sexy in his yellow and black Y-fronts and red knee socks. But give him time. After years of looking after the home and the kids, it may take a little time before he feels sexy in the bedroom.

5. The new family mealtimes are when they want it.

Have stuff ready to go from the fridge to the microwave. Children don't want food, they eat stuff – just heat it up and cram it in. If I see one more TV chef telling me that kids will eat pig's liver when you wrap it in pasta and serve it with vegetables in a cheese sauce, I'll drive down to the TV station and shove his hand-held blender where the sun don't shine. Don't those guys understand that, to a child, anything referred to as a vegetable must be gross? The only exception is a potato that has been chipped to the thinness of a matchstick, fried in stale oil, covered in salt and served in a red or yellow box. To a child, this is food. Mealtimes are a battlefield, with you wanting to feed them good things and them wanting to eat junk. Healthy nutrition is hard for a child to understand and trying to teach it to them is nearly as difficult as teaching them to eat with their mouth closed – their mouth acquires the appearance and sound of a cement mixer and they chew with their jaws open so wide that you can see the movement and colour of the food inside.

If your partner works late, eating meals together as a family goes out the window, as does your partner's dried-out dinner – and sometimes the plate. I've lost count of the times I've made dinner for around 7.30pm and was still keeping it warm at 9pm. By then, it's no longer a meal, but a dried-up waste of time and a statement not only of your feelings but also of your partner's lack of understanding. With the baby eating every few hours, their older brother or sister wanting something *now*, and your partner feeling that your kitchen is a café open twenty-four hours a day, you end up making more than just breakfast, lunch and dinner. With long working hours and the problems that come from running the house, the only hot meal you can have with your partner is in a restaurant and arranging that can give you a migraine.

A note about eating out with kids: DON'T! It's a minefield of problems. Keep remembering your last meal out when you didn't have kids. It'll give you a happy memory and a warm feeling towards restaurants. Only go out for a meal when you can get a babysitter for a few hours, or when your children are in their twenties. Restaurants could help by banning babies and children, or at least restricting times or setting aside special areas, like for smoking and non-smoking. Look, the last thing I want to see or put up with when I get the chance of a meal out is someone else's baby dribbling milk from a restaurant high chair, or someone's seven-year-old and his friend running around the tables being characters from *Star Wars*.

6. I will write a book on why women are the stronger sex.
Women are stronger. I know they are because they've told me so. I've been there and done it and I've wanted to

give up more often than a squaddie training with the SAS. I'm forty-two years old and for almost half of my adult life I've taken on the role traditionally done by women. If anyone looks after a baby full-time and wants to have more, one thing is for sure: they must be female. Maybe I'll write about my understanding of the stronger sex some day if, after reading this book, Caroline doesn't beat the hell out of me with a copy. Still, that's something to think about in the future.

7. I will find out the cost of buying a desert island for holidays exclusively for househusbands.

We're looking for time out with this rule, time for us, or time for a holiday. Have you had a holiday with your baby or children yet? Have you found out just how relaxing a holiday with a baby can be? You carry more stuff with you than you did when moving house and the journey by car, rail, sea or air has you as relaxed as someone taking their first parachute jump who finds that his parachute doesn't open. 'Oh joy! I'm effing well going to do this again!' Relief comes to the panicking jumper when his reserve parachute opens and to the househusband when they return home after the so-called holiday. As I've said before, how can you call it a holiday when your work comes with you?

8. I will try harder to win the lottery this year.

Most people dream about winning the lottery and, over a drink in the pub, many of them discuss what they'd do if they won the big one. OK, people say money doesn't make you happy and all the money in the world can't give you one more day of life when your time's up. But not having to make any more mortgage payments and buying a dream island for househusbands would make the bit between birth and death a lot easier.

9. I will relax the rule about children, sweets, chocolate and crisps.

We all want our children to stay off the sweets bandwagon for as long as possible, but something like chocolate has controlling power over some adults – and that power's doubled when it comes to a child. If Newton's apple had fallen with the force that draws a child to chocolate, it wouldn't have bounced on the grass but would have driven through the earth's crust and struck the core. It's not always a question of saying 'No' but of controlling when; we all fall into the chocolate-eating trap set for us by others. Yes, it's wrong, but remember: some rules stay, some rules go and others you may need to bend.

10. I will invent something that stops boys peeing over the back of the toilet seat.

If you have girls, this is not a problem, but getting a boy to pee into the potty or the toilet bowl and keep it on target is as likely as you having and enjoying sex on a Sunday morning. Mind you, 'target' is the wrong word. Anything is a target to a small boy with an inexperienced willy and a full bladder. To him, his wee is the water putting out the forest fire that he imagines is raging on the bathroom carpet, or his willy is a plasma laser based on planet Gozon firing at the evil Lord Zapmor's mighty army and they're everywhere. Yes, men and their tool bond at a young age. From peeing in the school toilets to see who can hit the urinal from the greatest distance, to holding the foreskin and having it inflate like a balloon, oh what fun little boys have.

Some of these rules may seem off the wall, but they have a chance of lasting longer than the first set. Rules which sound crazy – like 'I will try harder to win the lottery this year' – usually stand more chance than the one about trying to get a good sleep pattern for your baby.

Chapter 11

◉ 'Let's Do the Time Warp Again'

We can put up with a lot but the drip, drip, drip of even the smallest problems, along with the dragging length of some days… well, it takes a toll. You've had your head down for a few years, hoping not to get it shot off because of a wrong look or the wrong thing said. But now people around you are having ideas…

Nothing's said out loud, but you can feel it coming your way. If a child can pick up the sound of the biscuit or sweet tin opening from 300 yards away, a househusband can pick up his partner's mutterings about how maybe it's time to have another baby. After the years of looking after the first one, the thought of having another and doing it all over again makes your heart sink. This may give you the incentive to take the cheese grater from the kitchen drawer, go into the bathroom and, this time, do it properly.

It was only a few years ago – though it seems like a lifetime – that you were a more interesting person. You liked music, going out, talking about political ideals, banning the bomb and finding out why the 'Salter Duck' idea was left on the shelf.

I've been stuck in a baby-caring time warp for three years, and now my wife wants me to go though it all again, but this time I'll have not only the baby to cope with but also a four-year-old running around the place. For God's sake! No, I can't! Please tell me you're joking! Didn't you see the mess I was the first time round? Were my depression and sleepless nights invisible to everyone, or only to people who have two legs and are female?

I've got to get out of here; I've got to hit something. I know – I'll go down the pub and pick a fight with four big bastards. You know the type: the ones who always get loud and then, with a few drinks inside them, pick on people just for a laugh. Well, boys, your luck's in tonight, because a raving lunatic with three years of babysitting rage built up inside him is about to explode into your world.

As the evening sun went down, the misty orange glow from the thinly spread summer clouds seemed to wrap itself round the treetops, the contrast of the orange glow against the green grass seemed to turn it a deeper and richer green. Birds sang their last songs of the day, as the last moments of sunlight faded, and in what seemed the blink of an eye, all was calm and peaceful... No, it's OK. I'm not trying to turn this into a romantic novel, and you didn't pick up a different book when you returned from the toilet. I'm just trying to calm the chapter down. Sometimes, the feelings that come back when I write about them make me laugh, but some still hurt. The way this chapter started, I'd have done one of two things: run out of four-letter words, or exploded in the chair in front of the computer.

Whose decision is it?

Many families have more than one child and many women are happy to do the time warp again. But I was the one who was at home and would have to deal with the reality of the second baby. The hardest thing for me to get over was how little thought was, I felt, given to what the second-baby decision would mean for me. The pain I was in over the choice was, I thought, clear to see. The lack of understanding and sympathy for me left a hurt inside me that lasted for years. Those were my feelings, maybe women have them as well – I'm not sure. But if the man is at home looking after the babies, who should make that second-baby choice? Children become your life because at times they take so much out of it.

That was a hard time for me and not a time that I wanted to live through again. Was I asking too much from my wife by saying that having one child was enough? Was she asking too much of me by suggesting that I do it all again? I could hear the song from *The Rocky Horror Picture Show* playing over and over again in my head: 'Let's do the time warp again.' We talked over the different ways we could do it again. I could go back to work and pay for child-care, but Caroline's hours were as flexible as a brick, which meant I'd still be doing the child-care from 3.30pm until she got home between 8 and 8.30pm. In all honesty, I can think of only four times when I was at breaking point within our relationship, and three of them were after we had children. That's a sobering thought for anyone who thinks that a bad relationship can be made better by adding children, or that a good relationship won't have problems.

We did a lot of talking and a lot of not-talking, if you see what I mean. I love Caroline dearly, but she has a stubborn side that cannot be broken. No matter how much you put your case, if your partner is unwilling to see it, no argument or discussion will change things. I held my breath and played by the new house rule on the list: 'I will just put up with it.' Weak, yes, pitiful, yes, pathetic, yes. Any other choice, NO.

Baby: the sequel

Kate was born in October 1995. The build-up to the birth was hard. Caroline had to go through some tests, one of which was amniocentesis to check for Down's syndrome. I wasn't much help to her and I hold my hands up to that. I was looking after Aaron and the rest of the time I was worrying myself sick about how I was going to cope. I was drinking like a fish and unable to cope with all my feelings. Fuck 'em, fuck 'em all. I was hitting rock-bottom quicker than a traffic warden can slap on a parking-ticket. Have a drink and put up with it. I wanted an Out button, a button I could press to end the mess. No more me, no more problems, just no more. At the time this was going on in my little world, people all over the place were having a much harder time: people were being killed, children were getting their legs blown off by landmines. I only had to read a paper or watch the evening news to see thousands of other people having to deal with more shit than I had on my shovel. But for many people with children, when you're stuck inside four walls looking after a baby, that becomes your world. Unlike many, we had a home with our light, heating and food bills paid and were putting a little money away each month for future home improvements, but I couldn't shake my feelings of depression and it took Kate's birth to free me of some of my worries.

When Kate was born, everything went well. She was fine, and my worries about her health could go. But I was starting again, and this time I knew how hard the job of looking after a baby would be. People sometimes say that having two is as easy as looking after one. My friends, this is bollocks. You understand what's coming your way the second time round, that's for sure, but easier? No. 'Let's do the time warp again.' Back to bottle-feeding and baby food that always looks like mushy peas but comes in different colours. It had been a few years since I had to sterilise things for feeding Aaron but, like riding a bike, I hadn't forgotten how to do it.

The first day that Caroline went back to work and I was left on my own with the two children was a long day. I can't remember the day, or the date, or even the month, it's just in my memory as the Long Day.

Daddy's little helper

Right from when we brought Kate home, Aaron loved being around her, and many times he was a great help. He was only four but would play in front of Kate and show her his toys. Kate was different from Aaron as a baby. She was easier to get to sleep, which was a big help, and she didn't cry as much. Different baby and a different set of cards dealt out to the Charlton family this time.

The running around you do with two in the course of one day is an obstacle course: making feeds for the baby and dinner for the toddler, getting up and down stairs with a gate at the top and one at the bottom, and coping with locks on the cupboard doors, covers over the video player and power-socket safety covers. It could be a scene from a *Mission Impossible* film. Changing the baby upstairs, carrying her downstairs, opening the gate and holding the toddler's hand so he doesn't fall down the stairs.

We'd changed the bedrooms round, giving Kate Aaron's cot and small bedroom and putting Aaron in the larger back bedroom. He loved it. He now had a double bed, which must have felt the size of a football pitch. He loved having Kate put on his bed, propped up with pillows and ready for Aaron's show to begin. He talked away to her about his toys and showed her how Spiderman was going to save Teddy. The fact that Aaron was happy about having a baby sister was a lucky break for me, and I could get rid of a few more of my worries. It was still hard work and very much a full-time job –

two are much harder than only one. If the second baby's behaviour is better than the first's, it makes things a little easier, but if your first baby was an angel, the second may give you a shock.

Chapter 12

🛒 Shopping Battles: Making a List

With child-care comes the fact that there are only two places in which you can now be found, and they are the home and the supermarket.

We live in an age when shopping has become a science for both the shopper and the seller. The seller gives us the smell of warm bread flowing from the store's air vents and carefully chosen colour schemes for the floor and shelving. These subliminal inducements, along with the right lighting on the food counters making the meat and vegetables look their best, are meant to make us buy more and, for most of us, buy what we don't need. Bombarded by all this, the buyer also has to learn the science of paying for it, with cash, or with plastic store or bank cards. You can also become trapped in the 'buy me' cycle: two for the price of one, fifty bonus points if you get this now and free credit for a year.

There's an art to this selling game and millions of pounds are spent on getting you to part with your cash. I wonder if we could weave the smell of warm bread into the pages of this book, with scratch-and-sniff patches helping the reader to distinguish between smells they'll soon find in their home? Say, the smell of a milk feed brought back up over your third clean top of the day, or the smell of overripe goat's cheese? All this giving the reader a chance to smell the subtle differences between the smell of a filled nappy and the smell of a dead cat rotting in a plastic bag.

Some people see shopping as a type of therapy to cheer themselves up: 'I'm going to take the credit card out and cane it.' Rather than retail therapy, shopping as a househusband is much more along the lines of retail insanity. Having to shop has taken over from wanting to shop – from shops with wall-to-wall hi-fi goodies to shops with food and baby things. You have to push a trolley with wheels so old that they're as round as a fifty-pence piece. They squeak and wobble, even on the smooth floor of the supermarket and always seem to pull to the left. MOTs for shopping trolleys – what do you think? I mean, if your car squeaked that loudly and pulled to one side, wouldn't you want to get it seen to? So, let's write to our MPs and see if they'll take up the fight to get us better shopping trolleys. We could hold trolley rallies in supermarket car parks and cry battle slogans. 'We're sick of trolleys that pull to the left – we wanted a good one, but junk's all that's left' or 'We spend money in gross amounts, so why can't we have trolleys that don't rock or bounce?' Just one more – I'm on a roll: 'You make millions as we spend all our cash, and if we stopped, your business would crash.' Your shopping battles can start with the trolley and we haven't put the screaming baby in it yet.

Shopping can take over your whole day. You get to know the best times and days of the week to go, but forgetting the milk the first time means you have to trek back that afternoon. As you stand in the queue waiting to pay for the milk you forgot the first time, your baby is in your trolley, sucking the end of a French loaf. You got the French loaf to keep him quiet and happy, but you think: I only came back for milk. As you check through the items in the trolley, you add up the real cost of that second trip. You find toothpaste, whisky, peanut butter, wine, kitchen towels, a TV magazine (next week's), toilet cleaner, bread, beer, a pack of men's socks (six for the price of four) and a small plastic clip to put tea towels on.

Oh dear. Are you starting to add things to your trolley in the hope you won't have to come back again? Or because you're afraid that people will know that you're really only buying milk and will make judgements about you: how can you cope with a baby if you can't even remember to get milk? Are you getting cabin fever and making excuses just to get out of the house, because the drive will relax the baby and he can happily suck another piece of French bread in the shop? No, my friends, it's OK. Calm down. You're just going a little bit ga-ga.

Shopping amnesia

When you're locked in a house all day, with only shopping to get you out, the excitement is too much and you can forget things. You can start helping yourself by making shopping lists. Writing it down helps you remember; don't worry, we all do it. You'll be back at the shops tomorrow anyway, so you can always pick up then what you forget now. See, having a baby can send your brain so far out to lunch that you have to write 'Milk' on a piece of paper so that you remember to get it. But that's only part of it. The sad part is that shops are where you go to get out of the house.

Look, I'll admit to forgetting most of the things I've gone out for at times. What with pushing a pushchair round a store and holding a metal shopping basket in one hand, or having to push a trolley with wheels older than you are, your mind tends to wander. Sometimes you feel as helpless as driftwood floating on the sea as you get pushed around the store by other shoppers and have to put up with other people's kids using the aisles as running-tracks or as somewhere to try out their new roller-skates. And while you're getting pissed off with other people's children, you're bashed in the kidneys by some old girl reversing her electrically aided trolley. Then the pain in your side can have you thinking of other things to do in a supermarket, most of which you could go to prison for.

One evening, I drove to a late-night supermarket and found myself enjoying the freedom of shopping at 11pm at night without the kids. It was great: just me and a few other late-night shoppers enjoying the peace of a panic-free aisle. Panic-free because if you *did* have to walk backwards with your trolley because you'd gone past something which caught your eye, you had room to do it. Backwards trolley-pulling is almost impossible in the daytime because the queue reaches from the till back up the aisle to the frozen peas and the jars of pickled eggs.

Pickled eggs. That's an item I've never seen anyone buy. I've seen pickled eggs on the counters of fish and chip shops, and the same jar stands there unopened for years. I'm just thinking out loud here, guys, but who the hell buys pickled eggs, for God's sake? How the hell does anyone put their first pickled egg in their mouth? And after doing so, how are they able to keep that egg down? Then how can they go out in public and buy more? For me, to put a jar of pickled eggs in my shopping trolley would have the same embarrassment level as a teenager asking for condoms in a chemist's or having to be examined by a female doctor for haemorrhoids.

Unfortunately, you can't always do the shopping on the peaceful night-shift. Back to my daytime battle while shopping with a tired baby, a crazy trolley and some ignorant pigs who'd camouflaged themselves as shoppers. The enchanted sleeping beauty reclining in the baby seat had changed into a kicking, screaming, wriggling octopus, which I was trying to lock into the shopping trolley with the seat strap. I'd only just figured out how to get the pound coin in the slot and get the trolley moving, and now I had to figure out how this plastic restraining belt worked. Do you remember the day when you fitted the new baby seat in the car and how you seemed to have more straps than were in the instructions? After three hours, and with the baby seat still not fixed firmly (it's that word 'firmly' which has you pissed off), you read the instructions again. If the baby seat could be left just a little bit wiggly, all would be well. Your partner is calling the in-laws, telling them you're going to be late for dinner because you can't fit the baby's car seat and if the seat won't fit maybe it's a fault with the car and we need to buy a new car.

With that memory playing in your head, you start pulling hard at the trolley straps. You then see that both sides of the lock have to be pushed in at the same time, not easy with an octopus trying to get out while you do it. Oh, bollocks to this! You pull the straps through the trolley and tie them in a knot round the octopus. A few minutes later, the baby's strapped in and you're heading through the automatic doors into the magical world of shopping with a baby.

I reach into my back pocket for the list of things we need at the Charlton ranch. Oh hell, pocket was empty, list left under iron – I'd put it there so I wouldn't forget it. Brilliant as the plan was, it did not work, leaving me feeling that I should stick the list to my forehead or get a larger iron and leave it by the front door. If I tripped over it I'd remember the list and if I tripped over it and broke my neck at least I'd get out of doing the ironing.

The queue from hell

When you go round the shops with a baby, people may smile and help you if you need it. But if the baby's crying, forget about it. Without the list, things go downhill fast, because you have to walk up and down each aisle, looking at each item and hoping something will ring a bell. The trolley is pulling to the left and if that ignorant wanker in front of me doesn't put his trolley level with what he's buying so it's not across the aisle blocking the rest of us, I'll... Looks like another prison sentence in the making.

The octopus's crying and wiggling are getting worse. I have the chicken and the new Arnold Schwarzenegger video, but without the list it's hard to remember the rest. With the baby screaming and other shoppers openly staring at me, it's time to go. I grab some toilet rolls (you always need more toilet rolls with a family) and head for the checkout. I've never had much luck when it comes to picking the right queue – you know, the one that moves, where people pay in cash and don't want to get a store card while they pay. I know this type of happy moving queue is out there, because I've seen them: they're always to the left or right of me when I'm waiting in the queue from hell. When you see the checkout girl call for a price check you know your queue is going to move slowly. With the baby screaming, I am hoping for pity from my fellow shoppers, for them to say, 'All right mate, you go through – you've got enough on your plate with that baby.' No such luck. The price for the tin of tuna eventually gets back to the checkout, so the checkout starts to bleep again. Bread bleep, peas bleep, bath cleaner bleep, cheese bleep, nuts bleep, frozen chips bleep, milk (effing) bleep and potatoes. 'Excuse me, did you know that the potatoes are buy one, get one free?' asks the checkout girl. 'No, I didn't,' replies the customer, and you wish they'd put a rocket up their arse and get a move on. The next five minutes are spent waiting for the free bag of potatoes to turn up.

I'm looking for a kitchen cupboard to punch or a car door to head-butt. I feel a lot older than when I walked into the shop. Grass grows faster than this queue moves. Washing powder, I need washing powder. I have to leave the queue and pick up the main thing I'd come for. By the time I've pushed the trolley along the checkouts and up the aisle for it, I feel that my life is missing something. As I head back to the checkouts there seem to be more people queuing than before. Has the balloon gone up? Are people panic-buying because we're at war? Is Michael Jackson in the store, or has everyone decided to queue now, just to piss off the guy with the crying baby?

With my tolerance level reached, I remove the screaming octopus from the trolley, leave the trolley in the aisle and head back to the car – the shopping will have to wait. I might try later or wait until Caroline gets home from work and then do some late-night shopping.

Shopping with a baby or a toddler has its moments and until you have been the one with the crying baby, not the one looking on and criticising, you won't understand how a trip to the shops can go wrong – and go wrong very quickly.

A few more bits of helpful shopping advice:

If you can go shopping without the kids, do it.

If you have to use the bus or train to go shopping, don't go. Stay at home and drink your coffee without milk or sugar.

If it's something that just won't wait, make sure the changing-bag is full and pack something to eat and drink.

Have a game plan. Know what you want, where to get it, and how to get out.

This one is for you, dads. When the baby gets older and can sit in the supermarket trolley facing you, things don't get better. I'm sure the pain I get in my knees now is from years of walking with a toddler in a trolley. If you push the trolley without turning your body slightly to one side, those happy, kicking little feet can hit you right in the crotch. Shopping is never much fun, but having to walk round a shop with a groin that's throbbing after being kicked for the third time can make you feel like ending the trip before it's begun.

Just a thought for the readers who are doing full-time baby-care. Are your friends still calling you to see how you are doing, or to invite you to parties? No? Oh well, never mind, today treat yourself and do the shopping at a nearby M&S food hall. Treat yourself to a full-fat cream cake or a bread and butter pudding. They may be bad for you, but they can make you feel so good. Don't overdo it, though. Remember your body is a temple. Unfortunately, after years of looking after children, your temple will turn into a Greek ruin, with only you being able to recognise the good bits; your hair and six-pack will have gone. As you think about the old days as you pull out of the car park, you'll realise you've forgotten something.

Chapter 13

Bonding at the Chinese Takeaway

Well, here we are at Chapter 13. Many people think that the number thirteen is unlucky. The good news, dear friends, is that this is no longer the case for you: luck has nothing to do with it when you have children or are taking care of the baby.

Any day, any week, any time, you can have your world turned upside down. Your lucky rabbit's foot no longer works, fortune cookies only tell you that you're going on a journey (fat chance of that), and you walk under ladders in the hope that something different will happen in your day. Do you remember that song, 'Luck, Be a Lady Tonight'? Well, guys, my lady was the lucky one: she was out working while I was at home slowly turning into mush. Again, if you're having no problems with the baby and all is rosy in the garden, good luck to you. But I know that out there, somewhere, someone's reading this with questions still unanswered. He may have large bags under his red eyes from lack of sleep; he may be reading in the safety of a locked toilet, hoping to find some comfort. His baby-care books have been read and discarded on the floor and he's rubbed nearly all the fur off his lucky rabbit's foot.

A lot of what I've said may have made me seem distant from my children. Well, for a lot of the time, I was. I was just getting on with the job at hand and dealing with the routine of looking after the children. I love them dearly, but the panic and the anxiety I felt while looking after them didn't hit me just once, it hit me from all sides and with full rapid fire. One of the biggest problems and something which at no time before their birth did I consider would ever happen to me, was not bonding with the children when they were born. This was a bombshell. For years, people had told me that when their baby was born, love seemed to pour out from their bodies. 'You don't know true love until you have children.' 'It's a magical thing.' 'A bonding of the spirit – you're drawn to them and closer to them than anything in the world.'

Not for me. It just didn't happen. I remember standing waiting, after the birth, for some form of holy light to hit me. No, nothing yet. I remember being pleased that both mother and baby were fine, but I was tired and the feeling growing inside me – one I became very familiar with – was not a bonding love, but anxiety. I knew babies cried and that it wasn't going to be easy, and I'd been worrying about that for the nine months of the pregnancy, but the bonding and love thing was written in stone, wasn't it?

Every image you see of a mother or father looking into their baby's eyes shows this warm look of love. They've bonded, with an invisible, unbreakable bond. Let's see more pictures of real parents holding the baby, eyes wide open and with either a shocked look on their faces or an expression as blank as the pages in a Richard Whiteley joke book. Maybe this would help ease some people into the reality of the world of child-care.

Of all the things I have been going on about, the not-bonding thing is the one that hit me the hardest. I mean, how do you talk about it? 'That's OK mate, you may well not bond with your baby. Don't worry, the panic and the feeling of shitting yourself is normal for a lot of men, not this much-talked-about love thing.' I've heard of the baby blues. I don't know about you, but people talk about the blues as if they last for only a few weeks and only hit the mother. I was completely unprepared for the fact that the feeling of bonding wouldn't happen for five years. Look, I can't give you facts and statistics for the number of people and the time it takes for bonding to happen – I don't think the information is out there – but from the people I know and have talked to, there is a time gap and, as I said, it took me about five years. I can't remember the exact date but I know when and how it felt and I'll do my best to describe it for you in a second.

Bonding, or the lack of it, with their babies is one of the things people don't talk about openly. After all, it would be as welcome as a fart at a job interview to come out with it in front of your partner or the grandparents. People lie about it because facing up to it or talking about it is not the done thing, so we feel trapped in a mould which we expected to fit us and which we thought we'd feel comfortable with. Along with everything else you're going through with your baby, the biggest thing you thought would happen and would help you never took place. Can you think for one minute how much that hurts and how much it can make you doubt your ability to be a good parent?

One thing that helped me was the fact that I was thrown in the deep end of the child-care swimming pool. My feelings about the lack of bonding were put to one side, in the hope that they'd catch up later. Just doing the caring was dragging me down in the deep end so much that most of the time I was just happy to get a small gasp of freedom rather than think about bonding. When it's miserable, miserable and miserable, even a bad day can be seen as at least being a break from the routine.

The moment it was all worthwhile

'Come on, Alan, you said you were also going to write about some of the good times.' You're right, and I hope I can do that justice by describing one of the greatest days of my life.

It was one Saturday evening. I still can't remember the date because I'm trying to think back about six years. Aaron must have been coming up to his fifth birthday but just how close it was I don't know. Anyway, we had a friend staying with us for the weekend and were talking over old times with the aid of a few bottles of wine. We thought a Chinese takeaway was in order. I put my shoes on to go and pick it up and Aaron asked if he could come with me. 'All right,' I said. 'Let's get your coat and shoes on,' and within a few minutes we were off.

Aaron talked away as we walked. 'Daddy, why are the stars white? Why do my shoes feel floppy?' and 'Look, Daddy, I'm only going to walk on my toes, see?' OK, it may not have been deep and meaningful, but in his world these questions needed to be answered. We got to the takeaway, picked up our order and started for home. 'Daddy, can I have a cracker?' Aaron asked. (He meant a prawn cracker but 'prawn' is a hard word when you're young enough to want to know why stars are white and shoes feel floppy.)

I put the bag down on a garden wall and gave him a prawn cracker. I don't think it had time to touch the sides of his mouth. 'More please, Daddy.' 'OK,' I said, 'you can have some more when we get home.' Aaron smiled and took my hand. BANG! It hit me harder than a punch in the kidneys. His hand was so small that it fitted inside mine and my thumb went round his wrist. My hand went tight round his, not so it hurt him but strongly because it seemed to become part of him. The wave of feelings that hit me took me by surprise and I can't describe them to you now. I just cried. I was walking home with one hand holding a Chinese takeaway and the other locked on to the hand of my son. The tears were rolling down my face, and I could not, and did not want to, stop them. It was the greatest feeling of love and warmth I had ever felt in my life. I was so happy to feel it that I thought I'd burst. The saddest part was that it had taken so long to hit me.

When we got home, I couldn't talk about it. Aaron ran in and I left the food on the kitchen top and excused myself to go to the bathroom. This was my good feeling. It had happened to me at last. It was some years before I would talk about it with anyone.

Chapter 14

 **Money**

Before we go on, I'd like you to try this simple test. Go into the kitchen and fill a glass with water. Now hold out your hand and pour the water from the glass into it – try and hold as much as possible.

You'll see it slip through your fingers and flow over the sides of your palm. I should really have told you to do this outside, to avoid the mess that's now covering your floor but, while you're cleaning up that mess, think of this: this is how trying to hold on to money feels when you have a baby.

Money plays a large role in everyone's life and most of us feel we have something lacking in our bank balance. As children we are ruled by wanting sweets or the latest toy, with payment for the items coming from Mum or Dad. In the adult world, where we have to pay for everything from food to our own funerals, it's often hard to make ends meet, and adding babies to the money maths question only increases the distance the ends have to travel before they meet. Parents have to stretch some part of the family accounts at some time and it's harder than pulling on a pair of jeans which you tell yourself have shrunk in the wash. Nothing to do with your comfort-eating or the bottle of wine you drank with the ready-cooked curry for two you got from the supermarket. 'No, the jeans must have gone in a hot wash. Look, I *can* do them up, see?' The only thing people can see when you wear those jeans is that your love handles have become shopping bags. If you could stretch your shopping budget as much as you stretch your jeans, you could afford to go to Hawaii for a holiday this year.

'Born free, taxed to death' – a quote from someone I can't put a name to at the moment. Within a few weeks of the birth of your baby, you know that we aren't born free, because you are buying things since before the baby even came into the world. If you have a spare room, you're getting it ready by turning it into a nursery and bang goes a few hundred pounds. Add bedding, a cot and everything else that goes with having a baby and you can kiss goodbye to nearly a grand, and the baby's still inside its mother. Sorry, I still can't remember who said 'Born free, taxed to death,' but what do you think of this one? 'Conceived free, but you pay for that bit of pleasure until you die' – Alan Charlton.

The things you need for the baby add up, from clothes to milk and all the bits that are added to the list week by week. With your first baby it's harder because you buy everything the baby magazines say you need. For your second baby, the list is halved by re-using stuff from the first time round, such as bedding, clothes, the cot and the pushchair. Other bits, like the plastic baby bath with stand, travel cot, baby sleep mobile and the plastic things that turn into and fold out into other things, have all long gone.

Work, (no) rest and play

The real problem starts when couples begin to work out the cost of who stays at home and who goes back to work, or whether both of you go back to work, which means getting someone in full-time to look after the baby. If you choose that last option, you can kiss goodbye to most of the savings you've built up as a couple. The trouble is that the working hours of nurseries or child-minders don't cover the times needed for most working parents. The other option you may have, if they live near enough and are willing to help, is to rope in grandparents and friends to help. I think I've said this before, but I'll repeat it just in case my children read this book one day: if and when I ever become a grandparent, a snowball on a barbecue will have more chance than my children will have of me looking after their babies. Like a prisoner released from jail, I've done my time.

Back in the 1990s, when Caroline and I were working out the cost of the whole thing, my wages weren't enough for me to stay at work and to pay for full-time child-care. To make it work with my money, the choice was between part-time child-care or my taking over the child-care full-time. With Caroline paying the mortgage and all the bills for the house, it was going to be tight, but in the long term, her chances of higher pay were a lot better than mine.

The problem with paid child-care is, as I'm sure you have heard many people moan, the fact that many don't start before 8am and you're fined if you're late picking the baby up at 6pm. This is no good if your day starts at 6am so that you can miss the London traffic. Maybe nurseries could consider having something that works outside normal working hours, like a night safe in a bank, where parents can post the babies through a hole in the wall, with a machine which would log the time you dropped off the baby and stop overcharging. OK, this idea may not be right for some of you, but how realistic is asking your boss for a pay rise of between £25,000 and £35,000 to help with the cost of the baby? How likely do you think you'd be to get it? Not sure? Then for the answer rearrange these words: fly, pigs, might.

Of course, if money grows on the trees in your garden, you could have a live-in nanny and make plans to send the children to boarding school when they're six, if not before. If the money keeps coming in from the trees and oil is discovered flowing under the grass at the bottom of your garden, you may decide to have lots of kids running all over the place. Without the problems of the looking-after bit, you can enjoy the fun bits like bathtime, parties and giving them presents. You can go out shopping, not for food but for things you want, rather than need. You could go on shopping trips to New York, have a personal trainer, tanning weekends, big cars, fast cars and just do what you damn well like any time of the day. Who says money can't make you happy?

OK, back to the real world of paying for the sex you and your partner had which ended with the joy of new life. Pay as you go. That little phrase will ring a lot of bells for people with children. Why pay as you go? Because whenever you go, stay or return from somewhere or from doing something with a child, you pay for it. There's one point I've just got to make about taking children out. It isn't all about money. Something with a value of fifty pence can break your back and end the day with tears. If you take your child to see a show they've wanted to see for ages and take a couple of their friends as well, train, sweets and tickets will set you back £50. After the show you stop off for dinner at a burger restaurant, even though before you had children you said you'd never take your child to one – see how those rules of the house come back to haunt us?

After a day of trekking around town and with your feet feeling like they could heat the water in a footbath by themselves, you're on the final lap. Home is just fifteen minutes away, with a hot bath and cold beer waiting. Eighty quid has left your wallet, but the kids have had a great time and you're feeling good about the day. Then, as you pass a local shop, your child wants a can of drink and you say No, because you'll be home soon and they've had enough fizzy drinks today. The last five minutes walking from the shop to your front door can take away the enjoyment of the whole day. Just five minutes of crying and a child ungratefully dragging their feet has you vowing never to take them out again. You're focused now, and the things you're focused on are that hot bath and that cold beer. Instead of the joy of telling Mummy about the day, your ungrateful child cries about not having the drink they wanted. Your partner, having been through the same thing herself, looks into your eyes, sees the red mist forming in them and sends you to relax in the bathroom. The hot bath helps, but you change your plans for the evening. The beer can stay in the fridge, because you need a bottle of whisky from the late-night off-licence and a Chinese from the takeaway. The cost of the day has now rounded up to a neat £100!

The incredible thing about kids is that they will do this – cost more money in one day than you and your partner spend on each other in a month – then turn the whole day upside down in the last few minutes. But the following morning they will wake up with no memory of how the day ended and will be ready to start a new day of spending. You wake with a little bit of a hangover and have to fight with your jeans again.

The best things in life are free?

Now some of you may be thinking: come on, Alan, there are lots of things you can do that don't cost money. True, but every day you're at home you think of the monthly pay cheque you no longer get. If I could just stop thinking about that £900 not going into my bank every month, I could think of things which are free, such as painting, making a cake and playing games. Yes, I've got the *Hundred Things to Do on a Rainy Day* book as well.

Of course, going to the park is free, so you take your child to the park. If you're taking a baby, that's easy – they're happy feeding the ducks on the pond all day. For a child who's a little bit older and wants swings, slides and roundabouts, a few things can take away the 'free' aspect of the day. First, if that park's in

London and it's a weekend or the schools are on holiday, it will be packed. Just getting a ride on the swings means waiting for the spoilt kid who has no idea what taking turns means. After thirty minutes he still has his fat bottom stuck to the seat and it looks like he's staying there for the rest of the day. I know I shouldn't blame the kid for swinging all day and it would be fair to say his parent is at fault, but your day out has only just started and already your child's upset because he can't get on the swing. You lie to him, saying the boy isn't well, and anyway he was first, so let's go over and ride on the slide. After an hour of putting up with other kids pushing in and climbing up the wrong parts of the equipment, you round up your little soldier and head for home. The park may be free but it's a battleground when other children and parents are around and your child's upset about the fact that he couldn't go on all the rides and about the battles with the other children walking up the slide as he wanted to come down. It's not been a happy trip, so to make up for it, you head for the burger restaurant, where you're now seen more often than your lucky dip lottery ticket ends up in the dustbin. OK, the cost of the trip to the park comes from the burger meal and a toy to make up for the disappointment. I know as parents we shouldn't do it – you may say you won't do it – but I'm sure I'm right in saying you will. You can look on outings with your children as small costs and as part of the day-to-day buying that is just part of being a parent.

I hope some full-time mothers out there can empathise with this next point about money and being the one at home. Because I bring little or no money into the home, I have to ask for money to buy things and that hurts my ego. I'm sure this part of looking after the children at home gives us househusbands something in common with all our sisters doing the same thing. I've found it hard to deal with the fact that I still bring very little cash into the house, even though I do now have some free time because the children are at school.

When they were babies, it was impossible. I'm still looking after the children full-time, but between taking them to and fetching them from school I have more time to do the cleaning and look after the running of the house. I get the dinners, washing, do all the DIY and shopping, get the kids breakfasted and ready for school and take Caroline breakfast in bed every morning. Yes, every morning – in fact, for Lent one year she gave up breakfast in bed. But with all that my role entails, it's still unpaid. If you can get your hands on a few bits of part-time work, it's good to do it, just to put a little bit of your own cash in your pocket. It can be as little as £20, but it feels great.

As I said, I find it hard asking Caroline for extra cash; it feels like having to ask your boss for your wages every Friday, with them going over every hour that you've booked in on the time clock. I may feel this more strongly as a man, because society (well, the one I grew up in) sees men as the breadwinners. When the children were babies I had to give up working as a doorman at a club – one of the things I did in the evening to earn a bit of extra money. That was hard, because I enjoyed it, but I had no choice. As the main carer, you divide your time between the children and covering the time your partner is at work. You also have to deal with people who still think that being at home with the children isn't work.

The fact that money, or the lack of it, damages a lot of relationships even before children are brought into the household should be seen as a warning. But in the heat of passion, the fact that you can't afford to have a baby is the last thing on your mind. The woman imagines she's in bed with Richard Gere and the guy mentally goes over the names of the England football team again, to make the moment last a little bit longer. The extra money problems that result from a night of passion won't hit for another few months. Of course, there's no easy time to have children and everyone has their own, different views on the plans to make before starting a family.

Hopefully this book, or even just this chapter, has got your brain working overtime.

Money and paying for everything is a big one. When I first thought about this chapter and before I start ranting on again, let me show you how I wanted to do it. I hope it makes the point:

Chapter 14: Money
Whoosh! It's all bloody well gone, mate!

Chapter 15

What Time Do You Call This?

I'm sure you've heard this old saying before: How long is a piece of string? Here's one more: How long is your day?

When looking after a baby, you can no longer think of a 'working day'. I know I've been going on and on about how much time babies take up and how little time you have to yourself. But with you looking after the baby, your partner is under no pressure to come home; she can and does stay at work as long as she damn well likes. The length of your day can go up and down like a yo-yo and can seem to stretch out in front of you. You find yourself counting the minutes left on the clock until your partner gets home. The first few months are OK, working through it together, but soon – very soon – the plan to share time in the evening and on weekends falls apart. I would say that after the first year, the pressure seems to get turned up in terms of who does what and when, and the question of what time your partner will get home is answered less and less. The rights you feel you should have, as the one at home with the baby, disappear fast. How fast? Well, quicker than oral sex disappears from your life when your girlfriend becomes your wife.

Your partner's working hours will make a big difference to your day. If she leaves at 7am and doesn't come home until 6pm your working day is, obviously, longer than that of someone whose partner is home by 4pm. You may think that that's only two hours' difference and that I am being a little bit patronising with the simple maths, but when you're on your own with a baby those two hours can feel like a very long time.

Your dinner's in the oven

If your partner comes home at odd times, any routine you've put together for the children can break down because of the extra time you spend waiting for her. There's likely to be a battle over yet another burnt dinner or missed bedtime. The battlefield has your children in the middle, and you and your partner on either side of what can end up being a very high fence of problems. Anything from cooking the evening meal to planning bath- and bedtimes can be upset if your partner is late. The children don't like to go to bed until they've seen Mummy, but if Mummy's running late how long do you let them stay up? At times, I've had my children fed, bathed, teeth cleaned and ready for bed at 7.30pm, and we've still been waiting for Mummy at 9pm, with Mummy's dinner still in the oven, burnt to something that looks like old charcoal and the kids crying because I've laid down the law and said, 'No, it's nine o'clock, well past your bedtime, so off to bed.'

The atmosphere when your partner gets home will not be good – there's the smell of a well-burnt dinner for a start. Do you wait up to have a row about it, or have a drink, leave a note on the microwave saying, 'Dinner inside', and, unable to sleep and feeling pissed off and taken for granted, go to bed before she gets home? More than once my day has yo-yoed by – a few more hours and the stress of putting my children to bed crying has me feeling that I want to get out of the house, but that's not possible because you can't leave the children on their own.

Ladies, I'm not sure about this, but it may be different for women when their man comes home late. What I mean is, do the children miss Daddy as much as they miss the goodnight kiss and story from Mummy? I know couples where Mum puts the children to bed at a set time every night; if Dad's late, he just gets to kiss the children as they sleep. I know Caroline would have hated me saying, 'No, you're late, so don't go into the bedroom until the children are fast asleep. You can talk to them in the morning.' I'm not saying we'd have rowed about it, I know her too well – she'd have ignored me and gone into the kids' bedrooms anyway. (That reminds me: I'd better get a good bottle of wine, some flowers and a box of chocolates for when she reads this.) So, ladies, I'm sorry if I've got this wrong and if it feels the same for you. If your man keeps coming home late, get him to read this chapter or give him a copy of this book for his next birthday. You never know, it might help. He doesn't understand the stressful and frustrating day you've had, nor why his bad timekeeping can have you snapping at him like a small dog that's got its testicles trapped in a door.

For those of you who can't relate to this, look at it this way. Imagine that you've been working all day, whether writing a report in the office or putting up a wall on a building site. At the end of the day, your boss comes over and tells you to do it again. He rips up the report or takes a sledgehammer to the wall and says, 'Redo it.' You could tell him to shove the job as you leave the office or walk off site, but supposing you've got no choice but to stay and redo the day's work, with no warning and definitely no paid overtime? Are you still a happy puppy? If your partner's unaware of your problems, the battlefield starts when it's late in the day and neither of you feels like discussing them. If your partner comes home at a regular time, you can get into a routine – something which most people caring for children feel is very important. Again, with your partner out working, the person at home is clock-watching, counting the hours and minutes until their partner will come home and take some of the strain.

My working day with the children started at 7am. I might already have been up for some hours, because I hadn't been sleeping well or because one of the children woke me up by getting into our bed. Most mornings I was up before anybody else, owing to my apprehension about having to deal with another day and the problems that were about to start. Most mornings when the children were babies I dreaded the sound of the door closing as Caroline left to go to work, knowing that I wouldn't see her until 8 to 8.30pm. But many, many times, it was much later and I didn't know until I got a phone call from her at about 7.30pm, saying she was going to be late home. 'Going to be late? Ring me at 7.30 to tell me you're going to be late? Are you taking the piss or what? Any time after six o'clock is fucking late after a day of nappies, shit and vomit, for fuck's sake!' (I often said that to myself after I'd put the phone down.)

When your children are ill, your day will be longer and harder. Remember, babies don't give any warning of the problem as they sit at the kitchen table. No Defcon 3 or any other warning levels with a baby, just 'Splat!' as the vomit hits the tabletop and runs onto the floor. Once, my son and daughter were both ill at the same time, and I didn't get out of the house during daylight hours for five days. I had the routine of a vampire with insomnia, up all night and awake all day. Stir crazy, that's the phrase I'm looking for. I'm not talking about hospital ill, just the normal thing for children, when they're crying, hot and have spots. I was looking after the two of them; bathing Kate three times a day with some ointment from the doctors that you add to the bath to help ease the spots that had covered her little body. Aaron was getting better, but still had a temperature and wasn't feeling himself at all and, like Kate, all he wanted to do was cuddle up on the sofa with Daddy. The hands on all the clocks in the house moved much more slowly that week, I can tell you.

What about if your partner works away for long periods? How would you cope on your own for weeks, maybe months, at a time? I'm not in that position but I can feel for anyone who is. However, if your partner *is* away a lot, you must find that you have more control over your day. What I mean is that the rules you lay down can be stuck to more easily. If bedtime's 7.30pm for the children, you know you can stick to it because you're not waiting for your partner to get home. Again, I may have this wrong, not having been left on my own for weeks on end, but I've found that a consistent routine works better with babies than the on/off bedtime that a late-working partner can bring.

Thwarting timekeeping tantrums

When I first became a househusband, I didn't think at all about this business of getting home from work on time. But if your partner doesn't understand how important it is, given all the time you spend on your own at home with the children, the lack of respect you feel her attitude shows can drive a wedge between you. How you deal with it is up to you. Me, I gave in and just put up with Caroline's poor timekeeping, after years of feeling pissed off about it. I knew nothing would make her change. I deal with the routine as it is and try and keep the stress to a minimum.

She gets breakfast in bed, a freshly cooked evening meal most weekdays, ending with the washing up done by 9pm. I'm up every weekend to do the kids' breakfast, while she sleeps in until around 10.30am at the weekends, and has breakfast in bed at about 11am. You may feel that I'm a sad wanker for doing so much in the first place and you may be right. It's the fact that I do these things because I feel that I have no choice that feels like a rod for my back. People will probably criticise the way I've dealt with things or, should I say, haven't dealt with them. This working-day thing is a rod for anyone's back and if you feel I'm bitching too much about mine, that's because I have had to deal with it every day and I don't want you to go through it. So, if you're thinking about starting out as a househusband, you may wish to add timekeeping to your list of questions for your partner before you start.

Now, some years on and with the children at school, my life

is better. However, the children are home from school at 3.15pm, and if Caroline isn't home until 8.30pm that's still over five hours a day of cooking, feeding and looking after them. Add inset days and school holidays measured in weeks at a time… (Who needs six weeks for summer holidays? Maybe if Cliff Richard had been a househusband the song would have gone, 'We're all fucked off with this summer holiday, no more sleeping for a week or two!') With all this going on, what free time are you left with anyway? Free time? Who the hell gets that? Not much of that in my world. Some people bitch about only going out one night a week when they have children. *One night a week?* Try one a month – or, more likely, four a year.

This will make you laugh: one night Caroline said to me, 'You never used to worry about things. You've changed a lot.' Now, I know that you and I may never meet and we may or may not have bonded over the past hundred pages or so, but I do hope you're holding your sides after reading that comment. I'm sure I've heard that you can get a hernia from laughing too much. Having children turned my worry switch on and, like many people, I was worrying when I went to bed and still worrying when I got up. If it was a bad week and the shit had been hitting the fan, I'd dream worrying things. I'm sure this happens to women as well and it's not just a man thing. I hope it's not something that only I was plagued by. With what seemed like twenty hours a day taken up with thinking, worrying and looking after children, I was left with not much time for being me and, with the hours my wife worked, there was very little time left to be 'us'.

Most of this book has been written on bits of paper in the kitchen, bedroom and car over the past three years, then typed up at night, with daytime proofreading done after *Kilroy*. Finding time comes after a few years, which leaves you loving term time and dreading school holidays. So I'll get going and let you get back to your routine. Oh dear, I think I can hear your telephone ringing – your partner may be working late. Good luck.

Chapter 16

⊘ Saying No

How many of you remember the 1971 film *Escape from the Planet of the Apes*, in which Roddy McDowall and Kim Hunter travel back in time to give man an insight into his future? Anyway, the big news is that they're apes that can talk and, as you may imagine, they have a few problems.

The first is that they land on Earth in the 1970s, so some of the clothes they end up wearing are pretty crap. Still, the upside to this is that, with all the drugs people were putting up their noses or shooting into their arms in those days, two talking apes walking around the streets of a large city in flared trousers and tank tops… well, back in the 1970s you could get away with it. The upshot is that in a few thousand years the apes take over the Earth. All the dogs and cats die out from a strange illness and humans start keeping apes as pets. Yes, I know what you're thinking, but it's no stranger an idea than male seahorses giving birth. The pet apes end up being more like servants than pets – they start doing things around the house for their owners, getting their slippers, fetching the newspaper, running the bath, making dinner and doing the ironing. (Sounds familiar, doesn't it, guys?) Then, one day, one of the apes repeats a word he has heard many times, and he says, 'No.' A few thousand years later the humans blow the shit out of each other and the apes take over.

What's the link with looking after the children? Well, 'No' is the word most babies say after learning to say 'Mummy' and 'Daddy'. And it's a word you'll have to wave in the air from time to time to stop your little love bundle putting their hand in a hot oven, banging the glass door, or trying to put a crayon into a thirteen-amp wall socket. The level at which you'll enjoy this word rises as the baby becomes a toddler, and the toddler becomes a four-year-old who has no fear of banging glass doors or hitting windows with a toy. When he runs full speed at something while looking back over his shoulder, you tell him, 'No! Stop!' and feel as effective as hard, waxed toilet paper is at helping someone with diarrhoea.

So practise saying it now. Start by just repeating the word. Say 'No!' one hundred times every morning. Use the nine months of pregnancy to practise and then you can add different tones and volume levels to the word to see how hard and frantic you can make it sound. No, *No, NN-OO! NO!*

Little angels

We all understand that as babies grow they begin to test their surroundings. How much control you have or want to have over your child is your choice, but it's hard to take something back once you've given in.

Let me jump ahead a few years to make a point. It's harder to keep control or to insist on basic good behaviour if you've let things slip or if you don't give a damn any more. I once saw a mother happily stand by and watch her seven-year-old son kick the heads off a bed of flowers in a park. If the child thinks that's OK with Mummy around, what will he get up to when he's fourteen and out on his own?

Another time, I was at the dentist's and two young mothers were letting their two very young children run around the waiting room as if it were a playground. At one point the children went out the front door and into the street. The mothers didn't see this, because they had their backs to the door and were deep in conversation, but their children were out of the room for a good five minutes. I leant across and said that the children had gone outside. One of the mothers got up with the speed of a Reliant Robin going uphill and screamed for them to come back inside. A whack and a few choice swear words for each child, then they were plonked back, crying, in the waiting room and the mothers went back to their conversation.

If you're sitting in a dentist's waiting room with toothache, that's bad enough. But with two crying children who are as controllable as rabid dogs with their testicles caught on a barbed-wire fence... the aching became a throb. With the mothers showing no more interest, their children began to explore again. Under the chairs, on the chairs – if it wasn't fixed down it got lifted up and looked into. I found it hard to believe that people could allow that sort of public behaviour in their children. I don't think I've ever been so keen to leave a waiting room and get into the dentist's chair as when my name was called that time.

I confess that at the time of that incident I had no children and that, yes, I was like the person outside the boxing ring tutting disapprovingly. I hadn't yet walked in the shoes of a parent and those two mothers may not have been out of their houses for days and may not have seen each other in ages. After looking after my own children, I can see the problems, but basic common sense about seeing to the safety of your children, about the respect you should teach them and about having to demonstrate good behaviour every day, is a responsibility that parents have to carry at all times.

Years later, I was in a chemist's shop with my two children, getting a prescription filled. The pharmacy was at the back of the shop, with chairs for people to use while they waited. As we walked up to the counter, I told Aaron and Kate to sit still and wait on the chairs. I was taken aback when the young girl taking my prescription said how unusual it was to see two children doing that. She told me that most of them ran around picking things off the shelves and that she had to spend time putting things back after them.

Get the children to understand that when you say No you mean No, and that they stay in the waiting room or on the chair and don't move. No is a word for controlling and disciplining your child: by saying No to your child, you're teaching them basic rules for keeping safe and having good manners. With all my faults as a father, the one thing my children understand from me is that No means No. I feel I've built up trust with my children over the years and that we all feel the benefits of that trust. In the same way, if I tell them I'll do something for them I do it. My son's growing up fast and I need to trust him, from him going outside to play and not going further than I say, to not opening the front door to strangers. He'll soon be entering his teens, when the respect and trust we have for each other will really be tested. I'm confident that the trust will grow as he gets older.

Who knows, I could be heading for a big fall – I'm sure I can hear laughter from some of you out there with teenagers. Well, if I get it wrong, I'll do a second book and the working title could be *More Bollocks and Children*.

Nice and simple

I think that in the early years keeping it simple is a good idea. I'm not a fan of talking to small children as little adults, as I know adults do stupid things at times, from getting drunk and picking fights to starting wars, and, considering some of the adults I've met, I think it would be an insult to the thinking level of a child. What I mean by 'keeping it simple' is the basic rule of saying, 'No, don't put that in your mouth, darling. It's a plug and it can hurt you,' and removing the plug or the baby from harm's way. Then make a face as if you're sucking a lemon and make a yucky sound, and you'll get the point across. OK, you may have to repeat this many times, because the baby hasn't yet got much more brainpower than some adults you see outside a pub on a Saturday night, but when it comes to learning and understanding rules, at least a baby has its age as an excuse.

On the other hand, going over the top and shouting, 'Put the effing plug down!' will leave a one-year-old crying and confused. I know people get caught up with this idea that as a little adult your baby can understand you, but in fact they can't. Finding out why something is dangerous takes a long time, as does your own understanding of the possible dangers and outcomes of things you do as an adult.

There's no point in treating your baby as a little adult and explaining that a thirteen-amp plug is an electrical device that transfers electrical energy from the power station via the consumer unit into the home. And you'll only carry on digging yourself into a deeper hole with a longer explanation: 'So you see, Baby, the electricity lets Mummy and Daddy use things around the house like the Hoover, washing machine, iron, television and video, which we use to play all those videos you like. But if you put an electrical device into your mouth, it can hurt you – the naughty electricity can come into your body and can stop your heart beating, send your lungs into spasm and stop you breathing. Mummy and Daddy would be very upset and cry lots and lots.' (STOP!)

Sorry, this is too much information even for me. If I'm bored writing such a long explanation of why something is dangerous, what the hell is the baby going to think, having to listen to this verbal diarrhoea? It's just too much information. Repeating 'No' and making yucky sounds twenty times a day is bad enough. Repeating the above explanation more than twice is as boring and mind-numbing as... I'm sorry, I can't think, give me a minute.

OK, I'm back, refreshed by a nice cup of coffee and ready to come up with a few answers as to why giving a long explanation more than twice a day is more mind-numbing than watching the early-morning repeat of *Countdown*, peeling mushrooms, queuing on the M25, horse racing, *Big Brother*, *Celebrity Big Brother* or waiting on the phone and listening to the repeated message that 'You are being held in a queue. Your call is important to us. One of our advisers will be with you shortly.'

There comes a point at which we all get information overload. Babies and toddlers take in information about the world around them at an enormous rate – from how things feel and taste to making sense of what they hear and see. A long, detailed explanation of why they shouldn't do something comes across as a meaningless mumble from the nice face they're starting to know as the big thing that gives them milk and picks them up when they cry.

'No' and 'Yuck' do the job well for the first year and with all the information the baby has to get to grips with over the next few years, adding just a few more words in different tones gets the point across about what the baby or toddler can and can't do. It's not easy, and at times you can try and raise the level of conversation with your baby, but if the reply is a blank look and a soft, wet raspberry you know it's not time yet for the child to enjoy hearing you read Shakespeare.

It is frustrating educating a baby about the dangers around them. A baby only gets one crack at this life and, as a parent, you're the one plagued by all the dangers that can hurt or take that life away. You've only to see your child trip and fall towards a glass door to be, within a second, imagining the consequences: the blood, calling the ambulance, the child's panicky screams as they feel and taste the blood on their face, the panic of what to do or who to call, and the times you've said, 'Don't run in the house.' Just as you start your third imaginary heart attack, the child regains its footing and doesn't fall. Yes, this parenting thing keeps you on your toes and is a bloody laugh a minute.

Puppy parenting

After reading all the pitfalls about having children, you may feel like talking to your partner about getting a dog instead. I mean, a puppy is cute like a baby and for the first few months it also shits in the house or wees on your lap, but you don't have to buy it nappies, cots, high chairs or clothes, so it's cheaper than a baby. This sounds like a good idea – no bedtime or bathtime crying (OK, you do have to wash a dog, but you can do that in the garden with the hose and a bar of soap). You can stay at work and, with the money you save, buy that car you've always wanted. (If you're reading this in some future digital library, just replace 'dog' with 'ape' and you can stay with the action.)

Holidays. *Yes!* You can still go on holidays and have fun. Drop the dog off at the kennels on the way to the airport and then fly off to any country you like. If you like it hot, do a beach holiday; if you like good food, check out France or Italy; lie in in the mornings and have breakfast in bed; have sex on a Sunday morning. Stop it, Alan, stop it *now!* Oh hell, reality's come back into my world. What have I done with my life? I'm giving answers to problems I've had, for other people to use. This level of information is like gold dust!

Let's get back on track. For me, the dog thing is too late and I realise that some of you are in the same boat. But the dog came to mind because I once told a friend that when talking to a baby or talking to a dog, follow one simple rule – keep it simple.

As the years pass and the baby gets older, their understanding of what's going on around them takes some pretty big jumps, but none as big as their physical ability to do more. Before, you could sit them in the bouncy chair and their whole world was within arm's reach, or you could lay them on a mat with a mobile and a plastic mirror – all safe things to feel, see and put in their mouth. But the pressure of having to say 'No' begins when they start to crawl, stand up by holding the furniture and then start walking, and builds up to a point where you seem to be saying it every minute of the day. The baby's understanding of danger still registers only five on the puppy-dog scale of understanding, so you're constantly having to move things out of the way of this wobbly, walking, dribbling, object-sucking machine.

You put gates at the top and bottom of the stairs, but then keep trapping your fingers as you undo the child-safety latch and nearly break your neck as you trip while going through the top gate. And all the time, the little monster is looking to get through, climb up and crawl under things, stopping only to suck everything they can get their gums round. You put pillows over the corners of the fireplace so they don't bash their head. It works, but they can also use them as a teething ring or to help them get higher up and even onto the fireplace.

When they do put something in their mouth that hurts, or pull something off the chair and get a shock when it crashes to the floor, tears and screams fill the room. You comfort them, adding, 'I told you No.' A blank look and a raspberry, and off they go looking for – anything. Absolutely anything will do. You're always looking out for them, and the game is repeated every day…

Before I move on to the next chapter (and, guys, you're going to enjoy reading one part of it), I'd like to tell you a joke – I think it was a joke, I don't think it was put forward as a parenting aid.

A man tells his young son to stand on a table. The boy climbs up onto it, and the father tells him to turn round so his back is to his father, which he does. The father tells the boy, 'Fall backwards and I'll catch you.' The boy falls back and the father catches him. The boy enjoys the game and asks if he can do it again. The father says 'Yes,' so the boy gets back on the table. He falls backwards again, but this time the father doesn't catch him and he hits the floor hard. Crying, the boy looks up and asks his father why he didn't catch him. The father replies, 'Don't trust anyone – and if you do, never more than once.'

Chapter 17

✂ Graduation Day: The Vasectomy

There are many times in your life, starting with your education at school and maybe then at college or university, when you take exams and get some sort of qualification. And, like any course, training or life-training even, being a househusband has an end and its own type of graduation.

After years of hard work looking after the baby you can celebrate your graduation day. You can put letters after your name with pride. You've earned them. Mr Alan Charlton AHWP. It looks good on the CV and, as most people don't know what most letters after people's names stand for anyway, who the hell will work out that AHWP stands for A Househusband With Problems? It could be a code for when you meet other househusbands when you're out shopping or in the doctor's or dentist's waiting room, a secret handshake that only we know and understand. Maybe you could add a dot after the last letter for every year you've been doing the job. What about a secret tattoo on the palm of your left hand, say, a seahorse wearing dark glasses? I mean, we should get something, like Tony Hancock in one of his most famous comedy shows, *The Blood Donor*. After giving blood, Mr Hancock wants a badge as recognition of his efforts. 'Nothing much,' he says. 'Just a small badge, that's all, with a small inscription.' He then calls out in the voice and tone of a vicar at a Sunday service, 'He gave to others so that others may live.'

So, we need a point in time when you can do something that will change your life, maybe even more than having children did. The problem is finding that something and marking the day when you feel things are getting easier and the problems you had with looking after the baby aren't coming back. Your D-Day, your day for landing on the moon, something which ties in with the level of child-care problems you used to have. Got it! A vasectomy! That's a big enough change to any man's life for him to draw a line and say that any problems before that day are now in the past. From this day on, I won't have to change a nappy, clean a feeding-bottle or panic over not finding the Bonjela. After today, I'm free. OK, there's still the mortgage to pay, school holidays to deal with, the in-laws to keep happy, world peace or having to deal with falling property prices if an asteroid does hit the Earth. But after all you've been through, these problems are small potatoes – and I do mean small.

The preparation for my graduation as a certified househusband was to go to the doctor and get some information about having a vasectomy. Now, guys, I know some of you will be crossing your legs and shaking your heads. You may even be holding your love-sac through your trousers for comfort. Many men feel that their love-sac is too precious to put in the hands of a surgeon who might be having problems of his own, and might reduce his own stress by chopping the crap out of your lifelong playmates.

But we have to face the facts. How many babies do you want? The graduation day of the vasectomy is coming (not sure I should have used that word, 'coming') and a choice has to be made. Do you remember that old Health Education campaign which used posters of a heavily pregnant man? I think the caption was something like 'Would you be more careful if you were the one who got pregnant?' As the man, you're not going to get pregnant, but as the househusband you're going to be the one at home looking after the results. Can you go through it all again? Yes, you can use other forms of protection and you may feel that, with the sex life you enjoy at the moment, you have more chance of seeing the Loch Ness monster at a dinner party than of having sex more than once a month. If sex is that rare, you may feel that this is a good enough level of contraception. However, as a househusband you know just how much shit life can drop on your plate. You may have sex once in a blue moon but, like the bad guy Clint Eastwood pointed his gun at, 'Do you feel lucky?' After a few years of looking after a baby, who always wakes up at the most inconvenient times, sex may have lost its appeal anyway. That's something to look forward to if you haven't yet started a family or become a househusband.

Guys, I do know how you may feel about this idea, and before I had my vasectomy I had the same feelings and worries. But the only bad feelings you need have about the vasectomy are the ones in your head. I looked at it as an invitation to a party. Unlike after a normal party, when you feel your hangover's going to kill you, after this party you can move on and enjoy your role without the worry that you might have to do it all again. If you've had the operation already, I'm sure you'll agree that you felt great relief and freedom afterwards. So, I'll set down the facts and you can make up your own mind.

No turning back

After my visit to the doctor I was armed with a pocketful of leaflets and a form to read carefully, sign and take back; because it isn't always possible to reverse a vasectomy, you must view the operation as final. On my second visit to the doctor's, with the forms filled in and the look on my face that only a man who has been looking after children for many years can have, the doctor was happy to put my request to the hospital.

I was told it might be some time before I heard back, or got a date for the surgical procedure (that sounds better than 'operation' – I mean, I wasn't having a leg off) and I'd be given a date by post. To my amazement, the following week I got a letter saying they had a date for my vasectomy the following month. I rang back, confirmed that the date was fine and thanked them. That's funny, don't you think? I was thanking someone for letting me come and lie down on a table and have my love-sac cut open and part of me cut away. I mean, if someone kicked you in the bollocks as part of a heated argument, they'd be shocked if, as you fell to your knees in pain, you thanked them.

Having a date set did make the reality of the situation kick in, I can tell you. My hands got a little bit sweaty with each of the days I ticked off on the calendar.

Graduation Day. I got to the hospital about fifteen minutes before my given time and found the waiting room that had been set aside for the guys having their procedure that day. I don't think it was hot in the waiting room, I think it was just me radiating nervous heat. I was dying for a piss. I'd been about ten times that morning and I still felt the need to go again. I had time, so I found the men's toilet. To my shock, I couldn't find it. Not the men's, you understand, but you know, 'it'. The love-snake, Percy, the shank, the love-stick, the one-eyed monster, the sausage, the meat wagon. It had gone. My dick had gone.

Guys, you know how in the cold your package, instead of looking like a large and well-fed python lying across two boulders, turns into a tortoise's head which is moving back into its shell out of the cold? Well, when you are aware that in a few moments you'll be lying on an operating table with the surgeon hacking away and a couple of nurses looking at your shrunken package, 'small' is too big a word for the state your manhood is in. I heard my name being called and went back to the waiting room, where a nurse was waiting to take me to a room to get undressed, ready for the surgeon to come and see me. Should I tell her I no longer needed the procedure, because my dick and testicles had disappeared so far into my body that from now on I could piss sitting down?

The surgeon came into the changing room and talked the procedure over with me in more detail. It would be done under local anaesthetic, would be over in about fifteen minutes and I could go home after a thirty-minute rest.

'Are you sure you want to do this, Mr Charlton?' he asked, giving me one last chance to change my mind.

Yes, yes, fucking yes! I thought. 'Yes.'

'OK, Mr Charlton, just relax here for a few minutes [fat chance] and we'll call you through in a minute,' he said. Those few minutes of waiting passed more slowly than a late-night steak dinner with lots of potatoes passes through someone with chronic constipation. I was sitting on a chair wearing a hospital gown that didn't fit and feeling that they'd have to perform deep surgery to find the bits they hoped to snip. The changing-room curtain was pulled back and a nurse asked me to come with her. I tried not to make eye contact and I decided that I wouldn't make eye contact with anyone in the operating theatre, just in case I was ever walking down the road one day, or was in the pub, and was recognised by one of them. What a stupid thing to think at a time like that! Anyway, it's not your face they're going to be looking at. The surgeon is going to have his mind on how the hell he can work on something that has retracted so far into the patient's body. Just as I thought things couldn't get worse, I felt my ill-fitting gown open at the back so that my big fat white arse was on show to all behind me. I do hope this sight didn't put off any of the guys still in the waiting room and have them screaming and running for home.

'Hello, Alan,' said the surgeon. 'Please lie down and make yourself comfortable. Do you have any objection to Dr Bloggs staying in the room to observe the procedure?'

'No, that's OK,' I said, looking around to make sure the car park attendant and the lollipop lady from the zebra crossing in front of the school hadn't popped in for a look.

'You'll feel me moving things about for a bit, then you'll feel a little scratch as I inject the anaesthetic,' he said.

At the word 'inject' I think my body temperature went up by ten degrees. Then came the injection and before I could say to myself, 'This is going to hurt,' any pain had gone and I could feel nothing. A nurse talked to me about my work looking after the children, the weather and films we'd both seen. It did help, but all the same it was an odd feeling: I was numb from the waist down and someone who I'd only met a few minutes before, who was male, was working on something that few people have got their hands on so quickly. No first date with this guy, no going out for dinner, seeing a show or getting to know each other. Just grab and start cutting. So, while you can understand that the conversation with the nurse was helpful, my contributions did lack depth and meaning.

The funny, though obvious, thing with a local anaesthetic is the fact that you can see and hear all that goes on. Having a conversation with someone who is cutting into your body is surreal. I was talking about this to someone I know who also had his vasectomy under a local anaesthetic. He was chatting to the surgeon, who asked him what he did for a living. 'I'm a civil servant,' my friend replied. He knew the next question would be 'What department?' but with the surgeon cutting away at his manhood, saying he worked for the Inland Revenue didn't feel the right thing to do. I mean, trust and understanding are built up over years and he'd only met this guy a few minutes before. With a sharp knife and soft tissue so close together, what would *you* say?

'That's it, Alan, we're all done,' said the surgeon. 'Just sit up slowly and you can rest in the room next door.'

Firing blanks

The nurse helped me through to the room, told me to sit still for a few minutes and kindly went off to get me a drink. 'That's it,' I thought. 'It's over.' Getting there was the hard part. The operation was easy. After my rest I could get dressed, but before I went home one of the nurses talked me through the care I should take over the next few days. Wear loose clothing and take it easy for a few days because you'll have some swelling and bruising. Wait a few days before you have a bath and, when you do, taking salt baths will help with the healing.

I got dressed and decided to walk home. I could feel no pain so I didn't ring Caroline and ask her to come and pick me up. This was, as it turned out, not a good idea. I felt great walking back home, just felt happy that it was over, but when I got home Caroline said I should have rung her to pick me up. Having taken the day off work, she'd pick the kids up from school later, so I lay down on the sofa with a large whisky and relaxed.

I would recommend a vasectomy to any man who feels his family is large enough. It's over so quickly and truly the hardest part is getting yourself to the hospital. I did have fears about it beforehand, but it was just like your schooldays when friends tell you things – about having sex, or what the doctor does to you at a medical – that are simply not true. I remember many years ago standing in a queue with my friends, laughing nervously as we waited to get our BCG injection. For days beforehand, the kids at school had been saying that the needle was as thick as a pencil. By the time we were in the queue, the needle was up to the size of a drainpipe and you had to be held down by two doctors. Only after having the injection did we understand that what we'd been told in the playground was bollocks.

I will say this about the recovery time after the vasectomy – and this is a personal view, you understand. Instead of just taking it easy for a few days, going to bed for a few days should be the rule. With the local anaesthetic still in your love-sac you can't relate to the pounding your testicles have had. I mean, if you rested them on a table and got someone to hit them with a rolled-up newspaper, and then pull barbed wire across them, what sort of recovery time would you expect? As for loose clothing, by the time your testicles have stopped swelling, all your underpants feel tight, even the ones you've had for years and which have less support left in them than a pair of wet woollen swimming trunks. 'Some bruising' turns out to be your groin looking like someone has poured a bottle of dark-blue ink over you. As for your first bath after the op, be prepared. How can I put this? With your bum on the bottom of the bath, your love-sac will be floating on the surface, looking like a large black carrier bag.

It was a good ten days before my pants felt normal again, and then I had the joy of having to give a sample for the hospital to check the sperm count. You can do it manually (taking you back to your teenage years) or with help, but whichever way you do it you've got to get it in a plastic tube with an opening the size of a ten-pence piece. This is not easy only ten days after the procedure – it's like trying to pour water from a bucket into the top of a milk bottle that is lying on its side without spilling any. I had to give four samples before I got a letter from the hospital telling me that I'd graduated and was now firing only blanks.

This all took place some years ago. Since then I've talked to many people who've had a vasectomy, and all of them were pleased they'd had it done. So, if you're thinking about it, do it. But, please, do take a few days off afterwards. Before I end this jolly little tale, back to the name-calling I mentioned at the beginning of the chapter. You can now give yourself the nickname 'Jaffa'. Get the link? No? Well, you're now like a Jaffa orange: seedless.

Chapter 18

🐰 A Personal View

Well, we've covered a lot of ground. Most of these pages have been full of my feelings, ideas and problems, which may have given you the impression that I'm writing under a pseudonym and that my real name is Basil Fawlty.

I didn't want to write just a list of how you do things for the baby, as we all get over dealing with many of those problems very quickly. Finding the best way to feed and change a baby are things that you just have to get on and do. We may not like doing them at first and we may feel we're all fingers and thumbs, but they're part of the job and have to be done.

I wanted the book to be more about what people don't tell you. I find that many people, after I've talked to them, open up about their problems. I may have to start the ball rolling by saying something that I feel they can identify with, but then it turns out they share both my feelings and some of the problems I've had. It's hard when you have a bad time looking after a baby, but knowing you aren't the only one does help, which is why I've kept repeating the fact that others have the same problems.

I feel women have a better outlet for the problems they face in looking after a baby, mainly because they talk about them more openly, whether with other mothers at the school gates, or to the nurse at the clinic, or at the good old coffee morning at a friend's house. Men aren't good at this. Head down and get on with the job is more like it. Any feelings that they can't cope with are kicked into touch and the game of just getting on with it is resumed. The thing is, guys, every time you restart play and don't deal with the problems, you're starting with one less player in the game, so to speak.

Look, I can't tell you the right way to look after a baby and deal with family problems. One thing you'll have learnt by now is that a lot of the shit that fell onto my plate was of my own making. You're not me, and you may have family around you who can help, perhaps by babysitting one night a month so you can go out with your partner. You may have no problems in talking over your feelings with your partner or in being listened to. As for coping with many of the day-to-day problems, I tell you this: I wish I'd had the bottle, after I started looking after the baby, to walk into a mothers' group, put my case as a househusband and ask if I could join in.

The only real contact I'd had with another househusband before was with my friend Glenn, but he lived in Norfolk (home of the happy and quick-witted people). I spoke to him most weeks on the phone, and I think I have the bills somewhere to prove it. I needed to talk and let off steam to someone who'd understand. I wouldn't say all the phone calls were what most people would understand as communicating or as a conversation between adults. Sometimes it might just have been a noise coming down the phone line, unintelligible to anyone else, but I knew it was Glenn from the sighs, and I knew he was having a bad day. Other times we talked about what we'd been up to and, if our children let us, we might even finish a conversation without having to put the phone down quickly because one of the children had thrown up or pulled over something breakable. So I owe Glenn a lot, both for kicking me up the arse about writing this book and for the many times he just picked up the phone and listened.

What last bits of enlightenment can I give you to help you on your way? Well, the key to your health and well-being is probably not to have kids, and to win the lottery. However, as we all still want to have children despite it all, and as winning the lottery is unfortunately not very likely, then just don't be the one who stays at home. But if you have no choice and have to stay at home, then the answer is to buy a video camera. Film as much of the baby as you can, at birthdays and Christmas and of them just playing. I've got some great video footage of Aaron. One bit that I'm saving for when he brings girlfriends home shows him crying and screaming in his high chair. Happy days. Because of all the good bits you miss or don't feel happy about at the time, it's great later on to have a video that can make you smile.

When you're looking after a baby and your day is dragging on longer than an acceptance speech at the Oscars, it's hard to believe that this time will fly by. The hard part may be getting to grips with the changes each year brings and with how fast things move. Maybe the following summary will help you appreciate how fast it can all flash by.

'I want to have a baby.'

'I'm pregnant.'

'Let's change that nappy.'

'D-D-Daddy.'

'I'm pregnant again.'

'Oh Christ!'

'I love you, Daddy, bigger than big, and enormous times a thousand.' Kate, aged seven.

'Dad, are *The Simpsons* on tonight, and can I have a drink?' Aaron, aged eleven.

Looking back, time does fly. We can only hope it's a smooth ride, but maybe that's as likely as the England football team winning the World Cup, or finding a rabbit that uses a condom!